The Social Child

What helps babies and young children develop proficient social skills? How do children's early relationships and social interactions influence their future emotional resilience and wellbeing?

The Social Child thoughtfully discusses the key principles of children's social development alongside descriptions of everyday practice. It aims to provide the reader with a rich understanding of the social skills and relationships that children develop as well as their discovery of communication and language.

The book explores the importance of developing genuine, trusted and reciprocal relationships with babies and young children, and shows how a child's intrinsic drive to be social can be nourished and supported. Throughout the book, the author emphasises the importance of play in developing children's relationships and language skills and aims to help practitioners to:

- understand the factors that can help and hinder fundamental social processes for babies and young children;
- create secure and unconditional psychological and physical environments for children to practise their emerging language and communication skills;
- reflect on their own teaching methods to heighten their receptiveness to children's social attempts to communicate through effective observation and planning;
- engage with parents and carers to help support children's learning at home whilst maintaining the values of the family;
- celebrate the uniqueness of each child and provide learning experiences that are appropriate for individuals with particular learning needs, be they physical, emotional or cognitive, to ensure that every child has an equal opportunity to succeed.

Emphasising the importance of understanding the theory that underpins children's social development, this accessible text shows practitioners how they can use this knowledge to provide learning opportunities that nourish children's emerging communication and social skills.

Toni Buchan has been awarded a Masters in Educational Studies from Canterbury Christ Church University, and continues to lecture in Early Years and Child Development.

Foundations of Child Development
Series Editor: Pamela May

An understanding of child development is at the heart of good early years practice. The four books in this exciting new series each take a detailed look at a major strand of child development – cognitive, social, physical and emotional – and aim to provide practitioners with the knowledge and understanding they need to plan ways of working with children that are developmentally appropriate. Clearly linking theory to everyday practice they explain why practitioners teach in certain ways and show how they can provide learning experiences that will help children to become competent and enthusiastic learners. Whilst the series allows for an in-depth study of each of the four major areas of development individually, it also demonstrates that they are, in reality, intertwined and indivisible.

Titles in this series:

The Social Child

Laying the foundations of relationships and language

Toni Buchan

Routledge
Taylor & Francis Group

LONDON AND NEW YORK

First published 2013
by Routledge
2 Park Square, Milton Park, Abingdon, Oxon OX14 4RN

Simultaneously published in the USA and Canada
by Routledge
711 Third Avenue, New York, NY 10017

Routledge is an imprint of the Taylor & Francis Group, an informa business

British Library Cataloguing in Publication Data
A catalogue record for this book is available from the British Library

Library of Congress Cataloging in Publication Data
Buchan, Toni.
The social child : laying the foundations of relationships and language / Toni Buchan. -- Dual Edition.
pages cm
Includes bibliographical references and indexes.
1. Socialization. 2. Social learning. 3. Social interaction. I. Title.
HQ783.B83 2013
303.3'2--dc23
2012039580

ISBN: 978–0–415–52342–4 (hbk)
ISBN: 978–0–415–52343–1 (pbk)
ISBN: 978–0–203–55307–7 (ebk)

Typeset in Bembo and Frutiger
by Fakenham Prepress Solutions, Fakenham, Norfolk NR21 8NN

Printed and bound in Great Britain by
TJ International Ltd, Padstow, Cornwall

Contents

Acknowledgements

For the shared experience of our lives together so far, I dedicate this book to my mum.

I would like to thank Pam May for her unwavering belief, enthusiasm and support, especially during the writing of this book. I would also like to thank John May for his patience, good will and impromptu lunches. Thank you to both of them for providing me with a peaceful place in which to write.

Thank you also to my husband Stuart for his quiet and unconditional support, to my boys Connor and Lewis for the joy they bring to me and to the others with whom they are sharing their life experiences, and to my mum, for taking care of us all.

Thank you to all the children and parents who have given their permissions to use treasured photographs, and who have been willing to share their stories and quotes as part of the book. But, most of all, I would like to thank the children who continue to inspire so many of the Eureka moments of seeing the world through their eyes, and show us how the theory happens in practice.

Introduction to the series

Let us begin by considering two situations with which we are all probably familiar. Picture, if you will, a sandy beach. The sun is shining, there are gentle waves, little rock pools and a big cave. You have with you children aged six and three, a picnic, towels and buckets and spades. Having chosen your spot you settle down with a rug and a good book, occasionally advising about the construction of the moat for the sand castle or checking out the dragons in the cave. The children come back occasionally to eat or drink and there are the necessary breaks for toilets and ice creams. By 4pm everyone has had a perfect day; you included. No one has cried, there were no squabbles and the children are happily tired enough to ensure a good night's sleep. For days and weeks to come they remember the '*best holiday ever*' as they reminisce about the castles they constructed and the dragons they frightened.

Now, transfer these same two children to a local supermarket. Imagine the scene here. In my experience the situation starts badly as I issue the firm instruction '*not to touch anything*' as we enter the store, and rapidly goes downhill as one child finds the strawberry yoghurts but the other wants the blueberry ones. I want the mixed pack because they are on offer and a three-way dispute is quickly under way. The smaller child is transferred to the child seat in the trolley, kicking and wailing loudly, and mothers look at me with either sympathy or distaste as this noisy gang proceeds with the shopping. Matters are not helped by the sweets displayed at the checkout at child level, which this cross granny does not consider either of them has deserved.

Why are these two scenarios so very different? The answer lies in the ways that children are hard-wired to learn about their world and to make sense of it. This process is called child development. Children are born with a set of strategies and they apply these strategies wherever they find themselves. One of the ways children learn is by using their senses, so, they need to touch things that interest them to find out about them. That is fine when they are digging in the sand on the beach and collecting shells but not nearly as acceptable when investigating packets of crisps in a supermarket. Children are also hardwired to learn actively, that is, by exploring what is around them. Again, great when looking for dragons in caves but not such a helpful strategy around the aisles in a shop.

Figure I.1 *Checking out the dragons in the cave*

These books consider the strategies and other characteristics that all young children have and considers how they can be developed and strengthened in the course of young children's everyday learning.

This series of books is about the process of learning and not the content of learning. Each book describes a separate area of a young child's development and how their relationships and experiences affect the process of that development. Each of the four books takes one aspect and considers it in depth.

> *The Thinking Child: Laying the foundations of understanding and competence.* In this book Pam May considers children's cognitive and intellectual development.
> *The Growing Child: Laying the foundations of active learning and physical health.* In this book Clair Stevens considers children's physical and motor development.
> *The Social Child: Laying the foundations of relationships and language.* In this book I consider children's social and language development.
> *The Feeling Child: Laying the foundations of confidence and resilience.* In this book Maria Robinson considers children's emotional and behavioural development.

Although each book takes one strand of children's development and looks at it separately, this is purely for the purpose of study. In real life, of course, children use all aspects of their development together as they learn to sustain friendships and communicate, grow taller and stronger, deepen their understanding of concepts and morals and grow in self-confidence.

There are thought to be certain characteristics inherent in all children that enable development to proceed effectively. Two of these inborn characteristics, for example, are motivation and autonomy. They need to be matched by an environment which supports their expression and development. Children who thrive and learn well will find their innate characteristics supported by loving and knowledgeable adults in a challenging yet secure environment. This environment will respect the fact that children learn through first-hand experiences, through their senses and that they will usually be doing this actively. This is why the beach provides such an effective learning environment and the supermarket less so. On the beach children can use their strategies of active engagement. They are motivated by the exciting surroundings and can play with considerable freedom and autonomy. Here one can see that their curiosity and capability of finding out about the world are perfectly matched by their environment.

This series will examine these ideas in depth. Established and current research threads through and underpins all the practical suggestions offered here. A theory is no use in isolation; it must always link to what happens to children wherever they are, every day. This is why these books will give the practitioner a chance to consider what implications their reading may have on their practice as well as giving them sound, evidence-based understanding as to why certain ways of teaching and learning can be so successful.

Central to this series are some key beliefs about young children. These include the premise that:

- children are potentially strong and autonomous learners
- they need loving and sensitive adults to be their companions
- children's view of themselves is key to their success as learners
- play is a powerful mechanism that enables children to develop their understandings
- what children can do should be the starting point of their future learning.

Perhaps these ideas are summed up most clearly in the last of the NAEYC principles:

> Children's experiences shape their motivation and approaches to learning, such as persistence, initiative and flexibility; in turn these dispositions and behaviours affect their learning and development.[1]

These principles are about not *what* children learn but *how* they learn and, consequently, how they are best taught. They are reflected in the new Early Years Foundation Stage.[2]

The review of the EYFS by Dame Clare Tickell places much emphasis on the characteristics of effective learning that we considered above and it is these that we will be examining closely. Each book will discuss those characteristics which apply most closely to the strand of development being considered in the book but, of course, many of these will appear throughout the series. Each book will have chapters reflecting the EYFS emphasis on aspects of effective learning and in particular:

- play and exploration
- active learning
- creativity and critical thinking.

Other chapters will cover aspects of practice common to all settings such as observing children's learning, engaging with families and how to provide for the different learning styles of girls and boys. Finally there will be a chapter that critically examines the notion of school readiness. Each author will explore what it means to be 'school ready' and how we may best support Foundation stage children to take advantage of all that is on offer for them at key stage one.

Introduction to *The Social Child*

How often have we used the phrase 'he/she is just at that stage' to describe the response we have to a child's behaviour, demeanour or attitude? How frequently is this negatively intentioned? Would we ever use the same phrase to a grown adult? Chances are, probably not. Many social development theories, curricula, and our culture's underlying drive for measurement and assessment of children, rely on the use of identifying developmental stages.

Children are born to be social, and communicating is one of the fundamental blocks of their innate potential. Unlocking that potential depends on many connected aspects. These are not stages but a series of skills, attributes and values that can be gathered along the way. Not gathering these elements can hinder a person's life-long ability to function in relationships. Although every human is social, not everyone chooses to be sociable; social development is not a straight-line journey to the holy grail of social graces.

Language is the skill we use to convey an intended meaning effectively. It is the sister, daughter and mother of all relationships. It can be verbal and non-verbal, written, drawn, gestured or spoken. It is the symbolic representation of our thoughts for another person to experience and is central to our interactions with others. This book will uncover the myriad of ways in which we need to learn to speak, to listen and to respond to others in developing social competency and effective communication techniques and skills.

A fundamental skill of the practitioner and the adults around them is the recognition of the need to respect individual children enough to give them choices and options about who they want to be, and to give them plenty of practice at it. When a child is practising at being cross, and is in a tantrum after being asked to share with others, it can be a challenge for both the child and adults alike. The adult, often painfully aware of the appropriate social rules not yet gathered by the child, can choose from a range of responses they have learned – maybe with boundaries for behaviour, belligerence or embarrassment. The child, however, is experiencing strong emotions and is unsure how to either manage or verbalise them. Learning to emotionally recover from the upset, as they comes to terms with the rules of what social skills are appropriate, is not just a developmental stage, but an important skill, as yet unlearned.

This book, then, seeks to explore the range of social and language skills that can equip children with life skills which include:

- language
- listening
- vocabulary
- non-verbal language
- the mechanics of language
- taking turns
- empathy for others
- cooperating
- negotiating
- collaborating
- developing a sense of belonging
- developing a sense of identity
- trusting their own abilities
- building friendships and relationships
- conveying meaning.

The motivation for any child choosing to adopt a particular social skill is based on their being convinced of its social worth. Whitebread reflects how '*the journey has to be worth their while*'.[1] This book will acknowledge the significance of the interrelationship that children innately seek with the world around them. It will visit the emotional, physical and cognitive growth that supports a child's early use of language and influences their developing life-long social behaviours and relationship habits.

Most importantly, this book seeks to celebrate the curiosity and enthusiasm that accompanies many children's developing relationships with others.

CHAPTER 1

Setting the scene

'It's a bit tricky with my back facing the wrong way!'

Waking up to our four-year-old, Connor, at the side of the bed needing help before six o'clock in the morning can be a challenge. He is dressed in an orange T-shirt, green combat trousers and red Converse boots, trying to attach a Spiderman tie around his neck. It is the conundrum of his *'back facing the wrong way'* that wakes me fully as I am intrigued as to what he means – until I realise that he is referring to tying his tie. With a moment's longing for his earliest years, I am overawed to think of what he still does not know. This sends a wave of maternal comfort through me.

Later the same day, I reflect on the significance of our early morning scene. That orange T-shirt is the one he chooses to wear on his adventures with his granddad. The combat trousers are his 'work trousers', the ones he wears to help daddy chop wood, and the shoes are the 'weekend shoes' allowed as an alternative to his black school shoes. With no emerging sense of fashion, he has clothed himself in his dearest experiences. The Spiderman tie was his favourite Christmas present last year.

As his mother, the knowledge that he has these memories to inspire his dress sense is endearing, but the fact that he has such emotional attachments to his everyday life is far more precious.

As a practitioner, I can pick out the developmental significance of many aspects of our morning's conversation. Bruner describes how a child's social environment impacts on who they become. He says, *'Man is not a naked ape but a culture-clothed human being, hopelessly ineffective without the prosthesis provided by culture'*.[1]

Connor has already grasped some of the really tricky concepts. He has dressed in his own choice of clothes for a non-uniform day at school. He had been excited by the idea that by paying a pound to the teacher, she would let him wear his own clothes for a day. In return, she would send his money to buy a mosquito net for a child in a faraway place. He could repeat this verbatim to anyone interested; but does he have an understanding of what charity is? Is it uniform, non-uniform, money, malaria, Africa, famine? In fact, what are the special powers of Spiderman?

Without the vocabulary to describe his tie predicament, you could be forgiven for thinking his language ability lags behind his insatiable thirst for new cognitive understanding and experiences. But this would be a disservice to his social development. Even without the right word to hand, his desire to fulfil his purpose, and his implicit confidence in trying to make me understand his meaning using other words, clearly demonstrates a willingness to try. This drive to be social is hardwired, as is the flash of curiosity I felt, as his mother, to open my eyes to his request so early in the day.

What it is to be social

As humans, we are all predisposed to be social. By the term 'social', I mean we are driven to interact with the environment around us, in both a physical and a psychological way. We seek to sense its features, explore its possibilities and usefulness to us, and to gather information about it. This drive is never more pure than in a newborn baby, where the potential is unlimited by prior experience, undiluted by preconceptions or misconceptions and the balance of nature versus nurture is never again as even. Maria Robinson describes how *'Babies are primed to take an interest in their world so that they can begin the journey of finding out about themselves and the world about them'*.[2]

A debate continues about which of the born with, or 'nature' characteristics, and which of the 'nurture' factors, impact on our personalities. This ongoing debate could be considered to be the backbone for many social development theories over the decades. Perhaps the ideas Piaget had about children not being empty vessels to be filled with knowledge was not completely without relevance. Again, his theory of children as 'lone scientists' is not hard to marry to the curiosity and active momentum we see children use to explore the world.

Other theorists rely more on the interactive process of the infant experiencing their new world, and the child developing the social skills that will endure throughout its life. From the psychodynamic theories of Freud, the psychosocial theories of Erikson, the psychoanalytic ideas of Winnicott and Bion, and the social and language development theories of Vygotsky, there remains a common denominator. The human child needs to engage with its environment socially to establish the rules of its surroundings and culture. By developing communication and, later, language skills, the innate consequences increase the potential of what new knowledge becomes available to the child.

Why are we social?

Stephen Fry, a well-known literary enthusiast, explored the evolutionary rationale and biological mechanics of why and how humans evolved using speech as a primary mode of communication.[3] In the television programme, Professor Tomasello defined the origin of language as the point at which humans needed to collaborate and organise their cooperative efforts to gather food. Fry elaborated how, alongside this need to coordinate ourselves to achieve this primary purpose, there were other, unforeseen yet significant, benefits to communicating with speech. We became able to transmit our pasts, our stories and our own narratives to those in our worlds and across the generations.

Children's socialisation into their own culture is the process by which they learn what it means to be an adult human being within their society.[4] It is a complex gathering of understandings as to how our world operates. Bronfenbrenner's social model puts the child in the centre and layers the various influences on the child's socialisation into its culture like an onion.[5] This happens not in stages over time, or with one stage dependent on another being consolidated. These developments can happen concurrently and may not happen in a particular order and should be considered as a 'work in progress' process. What it does provide is an insight into the many influences that can potentially impact on our child's cognitive, emotional and psychological processes and can also offer some understanding about what being 'social' means. Schaffer highlights that it is via a child's interaction with the world and the relationships it has with the people in it that determines what the child learns to be significant, what it learns to be worth attending to, how it acquires language and labels, and in the process, develops ways of viewing itself in relation to the world. As Margaret Mead observed: '*Children learn to see themselves and what they do in relation to the people around them*'.[6]

Being sociable

Learning to be social and socially cooperative with others is a vital childhood task. Being sociable, however, is a personality choice for an individual. I know I feel at my most sociable when I am physically well, in company with similarly minded people with whom I share a distinct level of trust and whose company I enjoy, even if I do not directly share their beliefs and values. I like to feel confident to either conform or defend my own stance without social pressure, and, importantly, express my own views. In this situation I feel emotionally secure with them and am sure of their kindest intentions towards me. Crucially, I am able to choose to be sociable or not as I have agency. Davies stated how: '*To be social is an evolutionary fact, to be sociable is the free will bit*'.[7]

So do we give young children the same control, or agency, over their choices? The last child's birthday party our family were invited to was on a beautiful late autumn afternoon at the child's home. There were plenty of familiar friends for the children and adults alike, some lovely weather and a range of food sensitively selected to please all the attending children, including a themed birthday cake for the birthday child. The children were happily playing outside, using the garden to its fullest, climbing on the climbing frame, making dens, bouncing on the trampoline and using skipping ropes and balls. There was little conflict, lots of laughter, lots of chatter together as they made plans for their dens. Many of the parents even commented on how 'easy' a birthday party it was. It was then that the heavens opened, so indoors we all went for party games. Even before the end of 'Pass the parcel', a game well known by all the children, six of them were upset and crying. The change of child-led activity to being adult led had hijacked the children's sense of security and knowing about what being at *this* party meant. The parents had taken control and they had inadvertently undermined the children's agency to choose how to behave at the party.

Do our youngest children choose to be sociable with others of the same age, gender, religion or playgroup? Or are those choices determined by the adults who group together for support, social interaction and succour during our time raising and caring for young children?

It could be argued that young children cannot practically or socially make those kinds of choices. Many socialisation theories focus on the relationships within which a social interaction happens. If it is the adult's preference that determines the people that the children come into contact with outside the family, as well as determining the rules of how to behave appropriately when they get there, this might suggest a culture that offers children little acknowledgement of their individuality and their preferences in their earliest years. Is there a cultural predis-position to undervalue the worth of childhood, their right to receive respect from others and have agency over their choices? There are presumptions made about children, and what is best for them, throughout their childhood, but at what point do we, or should we, give them some agency over their choices? It is not our two year olds that have labelled the toddler's struggle for independence and to be understood, the 'terrible twos'. Who are they terrible for? Could it be that to lose our control over their choices, or have to reconcile our emotions to a place where we are not needed quite so much as when they are first born, make it terrible for *us*? These, and issues like them, will be explored throughout the contexts of the chapters ahead.

Choosing to be sociable

The underlying drive for the type of social interaction all humans seek is to have our own biological and perceived needs met. In the newborn child, the basic need is nurture for both their physical and psychological comfort whilst they are at their most physically vulnerable. From the rooting reflex (the ability to find the mother's breast as its immediate source of food just after delivery) to taking an active part in securing physical comfort, the child is driven to seek satisfaction. This is usually personified by noise making and crying for reassurance, which hopefully leads to physical closeness. Bion identified the psychological importance of swaddling a baby to provide it with a physical demonstration of security during its earliest interaction with its new environment.

In the pre-linguistic child, many parents and practitioners may hold a deficit or 'they don't do much' view of young children. This is underestimating the positive aspect of the child's development. What children are doing is developing responses to the emotional and sensory sensations they experience. They are experimenting with new emotions in response to experiences and limits, both imposed and perceived. They are consolidating an early knowledge of action and reaction. Gopnik and Meltzoff's 'cause and effect' theory concerned a baby's physical action and the result it got by kicking a mobile with its foot. The mobile repeatedly swung back, again and again. The child learned that this action would cause this response. For example, for a child with a temporary pattern of biting others, a common and completely understandable progression of behaviour for the youngest of children, who have not long moved past mouthing everything, the adult now needs a consistent and repeated response to change that behaviour. It is this same scientific 'behaviour cause and response effect' approach now applied to a social context. Thus the child gathers social cues and appropriateness of behaviour within their culture.

Relationships

The establishment of relationships is a life-long issue; the development of the social skills to make and sustain relationships are the foundations for every child's life experience. Relationships provide the context in which all of a child's psychological functions and learned emotional responses develop. It is the cultural appropriateness of the emotional response to events that determine the social behaviour linked to it in a given culture. As an example, Schaffer[8] cites a tribe of indigenous Eskimos who consciously do not accept or value aggression as a characteristic for their community. They indulge the very youngest of children and tolerate their emotional outbursts, what we might call 'tantrums'. From about two years old, all expressions of anger and rage are ignored, without exception, by the whole community. What this achieves is a next generation of children who learn the social rule not to respond aggressively to a negative emotion.

There is much theory surrounding the significance of a child's earliest relationships, and the blueprint that these critical relationships generate for interactional behaviour later in life. From Trevarthen's theory of 'intersubjectivity',[9] to Schaffer's 'reciprocity', and then, more recently, Gerhardt's 'dance of mutual responsiveness',[10] all allude to the critical importance of the mother/child relationship. The fundamental social skills that are founded in this relationship and developed at this early age are pivotal to a child's later emotional security, its sense of self-esteem and self-acceptance. These characteristics in a person can impact on their 'social capital' later in life. This concept, along with the many theories that underpin it, will be further explored in Chapters 3 and 4.

Relationship with self

Maria Robinson suggests that the development of being conscious of oneself and the wider world begins with the care that a child receives from attentive adults.[11]

In young children, this early sense of self-awareness and self-identity is a very fluid state, with many factors impacting on it. Eliot suggests that the young child's brain is anything but hardwired, and although their drive to be social with the world around them is integral, the potency of the effect the wider world has on the child's sense of belonging and sense of identity is not fixed in the early years.[12]

Figure 1.1 *Seeing yourself*

However we have to be careful of using such terms. As cognitive neuroscientist, Giordana Grossi states, '*terms like hardwired – on loan from computer science where it refers to fixedness – translate poorly to the domain of neural circuits that change and learn throughout life, indeed, in response to life*'.[13]

Along with attentive and responsive adults, the child's need to imitate, practise and consolidate their newly acquired knowledge about their new social world is paramount. This is why role play, fantasy play, open-ended resources and time are so important in children's play. Anything that provides a selection of choice, that does not limit imagination and encourages self-expression, can heighten their interest, their engagement and deepen children's self-awareness. Maslow's hierarchy of needs alludes to how a grounded sense of belonging and identity creates a foundation for a person's self-actualisation.[14] By the term self-actualisation, Maslow means a state where a person has a sense of ease with their own self, a certain self-awareness and identity and understanding of how they may be perceived by others. This concept is a sophisticated one, not least because the process to become self-actualised is interactive in relation to the world and people around us. Mead describes how children become aware of *'the significant other'*,[15] often the main care-giver initially, learning to take on their roles and gradually becoming aware of themselves in relation to others. The final stage of becoming an adult self is becoming aware of 'the generalised other', or being able to imagine being many 'others' in many situations.

Relationships with friends

In 2009 Layard and Dunn conducted a UK national review called *The Good Childhood Inquiry*,[16] asking a wide cross-section of our children what they considered constituted a good childhood and contributed to their happiness. Right at the top were relationships with their friends, and being listened to and understood by the adults in their lives. Above lots of money or toys and gadgets, success or popularity, their ideas about enjoying mutually responsive relationships was more important. This sentiment has not changed in nearly thirty years, through a hugely capitalistic 1980s and a perceived slippery slope to insular individualism during the 1990s and into the new century. Bronwyn Davies discovered how adults assume that the reason friendships develop is that people like each other.[17] In contrast, children see proximity and being close to someone as the first and basic element of friendship. Children, as they develop their socialised self through childhood, understand that forming friendships helps to set up a working knowledge of who you are, providing opportunities to practise social and language concepts with a peer group, outside adult authority. Newson and Newson offered: *'school is the context which crystallises the child's transformation into a social creature, which formalises his experience of the peer group and of outside adult authority'*.[18]

Communication and language

The constructions and understandings of what communicating, acquiring and using language means, and how it develops in a human, continues to be the subject of many researchers, from many disciplines. One such set of researchers, Devlin and Price, have used modern technological advances to better understand how language develops in the brain. Price described, in a BBC programme, how the brain's *'language processes integrates all our sensory sources cognitively and then co-ordinates a response to it. This interaction of brain to environment is hardwired and integral'*.[19]

So, if acquiring language can involve collecting all the sensory information an experience or sensation can offer us, our brains assimilating and classifying the information and offering a response to it, then we can begin to understand how our knowledge about how things work, grows. Think about it: have you ever seen a baby younger than about ten months scratch an itch? It does not mean they have not experienced a tickle, or an abrasive surface or sat on itchy grass. Only when their brains and neural maturity allows the sensation to be cognitively processed as to what it means, locate it on their bodies and initiate a separate and purposeful action to remedy it with a scratch, can the brain file it away in the 'can do it' drawer. The same is true of our early communication with children. Our use of 'baby talk' does not stop because the baby does not comprehend what is being said and cannot answer back. The best we can hope for from a newborn is maybe an engagement of their attention or a spark of mutual recognition. Nonetheless, we persist in immersing the new child in a world of simplified, adapted language during this time. As adult inhabitants of the world our children live in, we have experienced the value of having a competent grasp of language and symbolic representation. A child's ability to access the world it will experience during its life is also enhanced by its grasp of the meaning of symbols and language.

Later on, ludic or playful language with young children continues to be a source of language practice for children as well as a source of delight for adults and children alike. If you have ever heard a child repeatedly call a bulldozer a *'dullbozer'*, refer to that notorious Star Wars character as *'Daft Vader'*, or work hard to find sounds that rhyme with *'bum'*, and you have chosen not to correct, chide or adapt, you will know why. How young children establish modes of communication and develop language proficiency, the theories surrounding it and the ways they learn to use it socially will be explored through the chapters to follow.

Relationships and language

It is language and the use of language to express our feelings that connects us to other people and gives us social proficiency. It is not by chance that social and emotional development have been linked together in every version of Early Years curricula for the last thirty years. But there is a silent cousin to using language, and that is listening. Speaking and listening are the fundamental skills of becoming competent communicators, and acquiring the essential skills of establishing friendships and relationships. Do we really listen to our children? Not just listen to their noises in response to our requests or instructions, but do we hear what they have to say? Conversely, before they can talk, young children rely on reading body language, but can we read theirs or have we discarded the skill of consciously registering the physical signals others give us to convey what they mean? Surprisingly young children can articulate difficult feelings and convey complex ideas, but do we listen closely enough to hear them?

Jacob said, '*How long before we see granddad?*'

His mother replied, '*Five sleeps*'.

It is not the complex concept of the passing of time that Jacob has not grasped; it is the imposed adult language to describe it that still eludes him.

Chapter 5 and 6 explore the vital communication techniques we could all actively practise.

In the wider world

To return to the idea of whether we undervalue the worth of childhood is a prominent contemporary discussion. Many historical theorists identified children as deficit beings, as passive, disadvantaged and isolated; with childhood itself seen as a negative and vulnerable life stage. But ask any child of a baby boomer (someone born in the post World War II years), their childhood experience will often be full of nostalgic memories of freedom, lack of responsibility, trips out and summer days. The way our post-war parents raised us has established a distinctly different trend from the modern childhood, one which has its own demons to contend with.

In their book *Consuming Children*, Kenway and Bullen acknowledge the central role of the consumer-media culture on our next generation and reflect on the possibilities and predicaments it can present for today's children, parents and educators. Postman describes the end of childhood, and firmly places the blame at the feet of the media, and the printed word.[20] But Postman's version of childhood relies on a nostalgic and romantic memory of our own childhoods, one that he describes as '*a growth of sentiment about childhood*'.[21] This nostalgic history of childhood portrays our collective sense of powerlessness over children and conveys that there once was a golden age of childhood in which individual adults were in control and that children were under control. It is this perception of an adult's lack of control over children, and our need to have a reason for it, that renders all media, including electronic media and commercialism, to be perceived as having a predominantly negative influence on children. Others see the opportunities and possibilities of these mediums to be enjoyed by all children as inevitable and empowering for the next generation. Tapscott refers to, what he calls, the savvy N–Geners who can exist in the real and virtual worlds simultaneously and have never felt limited by communication modes such as sending a facsimile, let alone a telegram.[22] While Kirkham writes of '*The expanding virtual world of information technology threatening to engulf our sense of reality*'.[23]

But the media and digitally interactive world are already here, and both communicate with our children on an individual and engaging level. For children, it is an integral part of the way their world operates, and they will develop understanding of it as they encounter it. As for us, already adult, we have to undo our learned knowledge so far, to accommodate new information about something outside the experiences we encountered as children. The fact that both the media and the internet, and particularly the social networking phenomenon of recent years, encompass and challenge our basic understandings of relationships, language and being sociable mean that we, as adults, have a reboot process to go through. The Byron Review found that there was '*a generational digital divide*' and that '*Everyone has a role to play in empowering children to stay safe while they enjoy these new technologies, just as it is everyone's responsibility to keep children safe in the non-digital world.*'[24]

As for the consumer culture that influences our children, there is no doubt that young children find visually stimulating gadgets attractive, for the same reason that I am drawn to a new pair of shoes or pictures of a tropical holiday. What young children cannot discern is the power of that visual imagery and the lack of truth attached to it. Picture the Christmas morning when the 'as advertised' latest craze toy is unwrapped only to find out that it does not fly around the room without human hand. Would you legislate against this kind of disappointment? Later chapters will consider the impact of real and virtual worlds, both tangible and intangible, that our children engage in and the levels of control we, as adults, assert over them.

CHAPTER 2

Play, imitation and exploration

'My tongue is all freckled!'

Emily, three years old

As practitioners and educators, we always tend to place and protect play as the first priority for our youngest children. We come to experience and understand the importance of play for children as the vehicle for so many cognitive, social and emotional, language and growth developments. From the valuable work we do with children, as well as the frameworks and guidelines that inform us in our work, play is paramount as the most effective way our children practise possibilities, revisit things they have experienced and reconcile and express how they feel about things. We have playtime, playgrounds, soft play, playrooms and play days. But all these things are adult words, from our adult perspectives and for our management of the time we spend with children, and not always purely for or led by children themselves.

As adults we are desensitised from many of our own sensory messages, having seen, experienced or categorised what a specific sensation means previously. We do not always consciously register the location of an itch, we do not always see periphery items in our vision and, as adults, often take up hobbies that seek to reconnect us with our senses be they thrill-seeking, meditative or tactile. A baby's senses are much more heightened than our own; they need to be to cope with the new environment they find themselves in.

By reversing the order of play, imitation and exploration, we can, perhaps, highlight the links between the three more competently. If the newborn baby was born into a social vacuum, with its immediate biological needs taken care of and then left, it would have only its senses to rely on in order to explore its environment and to make sense of where it was. This would be a cruel and unimaginable thing to do, but it is the sensory exploration of its surroundings that is innate, first and foremost.

Past this most vulnerable early physical stage, as newborns adjust to life on the outside they rely on the smell of us, the comforting closeness of us and our care of their needs. As they become increasingly reassured with being able to rely on us to provide their basic needs and their biological maturity progresses, babies will begin to explore the things and the immediate world around them. We all know babies will put everything in their mouths, and as their bodies strengthen physically, they will reach for everything they can see and seek to explore all they are curious about with those senses they were born with.

As babies grow bigger, they rely on their maturing senses to gather new information about the environment they are in, with each of the senses being equally important. Why does the eighteen-month-old child, who has learnt that pulling the hair of another person can get a strong vocal response, always let go when you cover their eyes and make no noise? By restricting the sensory messages a child receives, regaining these senses becomes more important than feeling the hair or seeking to evoke your expression of the painful effect of their action. To a child of this age, its senses are everything. But what influences the response the child makes to the sensory information it receives? This is when imitation becomes so important.

Using imitation to develop relationships

From a child's early smile of recognition to the early repeated noises that begin to correspond to particular actions or things, babies and young children are learning that symbols can represent other things. Long before they can mark-make and write, children are cognitively mature enough to understand that movement and noise can signify, to an interested other, that something is being communicated. We do not ignore the babbles or pointing of a non-speaking toddler; instead we attempt to interpret what they mean and often provide positive acknowledgement and recognition of their efforts.

With such satisfying emotional paybacks and responses for effort, children are both innately and extrinsically motivated to continue trying. Even for children without consistent and positive responses from adults and others around them, the child's intrinsic drive to make themselves understood, as a social being, will make them continue to try. It is the response they receive that sets the patterns for social behaviour they develop for future relationships. The child begins to relate to the world, and the others in it.

Theoretically, Skinner's behaviourist models of learning made important contributions to the understanding of how, through the observation and imitation of the behaviour of others, we become conditioned into the rules of behaviour within a society.[1] These learned behaviours are influenced by a wide range of external rewards and reinforcements. But these findings were inspired by experiments conducted on dogs by Pavlov, and although they have value in describing how living beings can exist communally, they assume a fixed idea that animals and human children learn in similar ways. They do not reflect on the interactional world of the human child. It is the relational context of each child's individual experience to others, and their early emotions about those experiences, that provide their points of reference for many of the social skills they go on to develop. For this, imitation is key. We are the gatekeepers to the responses a child has to their world; our response to them on every level is significant. The points of reference we provide in our responses to them, their actions and their noises and their attempts at communication, become the blueprint for their first understandings of their selves, their world and how they fit into it.

Socially emotional responses

The responses I refer to are not the comforting noises we may make to a crying child, the physical cuddle we offer or giving children the appropriate emotional language to aid and develop their own unfettered expression of emotions. These are all valuable responses as learnt social skills for certain situations, ones which children can and often will learn as the skills become meaningful and useful to them. Instead, I am referring to the unconditional concern any human would have for any other living being, and the actions and reactions that these prompt in us as humans. This is often referred to as empathy. How do we encourage and nurture a child's capacity for kindness and their concern for others? How do you inspire this key social skill in children?

It is difficult to unravel the significance of empathy in relation to successful life relationships. But not having it, being unable to see another's point of view, understand and value their stance or not being able to socially and emotionally respond to another, can inhibit many life skills. Collaboration and teamwork become fragmented, successful negotiation becomes conflict, resolution and relationships can become tainted by power or insincerity. This is because of the inherent distrust of intention.

Empathy is arguably an unteachable skill; it is only genuinely gained as a by-product of a child relating to the response made by one to another's actions and situations. First, what they see must make sense to the child, and second, they must have their own response to it on behalf of the 'other' involved. Only by having strong emotional responses to what they see around them can these responses be internalised and referred to later as their own. I am careful to isolate the actions, reactions and consequences from the individual here, because children, as the newer members of their community, imitate the actions, language and behaviour of those around them, including us as practitioners. This process, in itself, does not ensure an empathic nature but, as adults, we have a duty to provide scenes and opportunities for children that are meaningful, connected and tangible.

In their innate drive to socialise, being able to see and hear is particularly prominent as it motivates them to imitate what they see around them and mimic what they hear. The significance of imitation cannot be underplayed as we consider the emerging language skills of young children. Consider the following interaction:

> Adult to two-year-old child: '*But it is dinner time, I know you have finished but I would like you to sit up at the table while we all finish as well!*' (gestured with a flat hand point towards the child, whilst looking clearly in the direction of the child)

Child to adult: '*Me do not want to have dis 'scussion wiv ou right now!*' (head tilted away from eye contact with the adult, but a firm gesture of both hands flat and jerked downwards in the direction of the adult, mimicking the adult's gesture.)

Socially speaking

So if we know that children use their senses to explore their physical environment and their relationship with it, and they rely on imitation to practise the symbols, language and behaviours of their own culture, where does this leave play and how significant is it for young children and their social development?

If you have worked in childcare services over the last thirty years you would have found it difficult to avoid the indoctrination of the importance of learning through play. Educational models such as Froebel, Montessori and Steiner all reinforced its significance, with Macmillan and Isaacs both placing evidence on children experiencing related things first hand. Isaacs, in particular, forged ahead with the idea of 'free flow' play, a concept of children determining the order and significance of what they encountered and what relevance they attached to it. Often now used in practice to describe leaving the door between indoor and outdoor spaces open, the original concept was about allowing children freedom of choice and agency to decide what and how they want to use to help them make new sense of their world.

Figure 2.1 *Choice and agency*

In their chapter 'Is it OK to Play?', Hirst and Nutbrown offer us a comprehensive link from the theory of the importance of play to the justified use of play in our current curricula. To borrow a quote from Tricia David, who succinctly states the value of contemporary play:

> During play, children are free to make choices and to follow interests, are self motivated, engage in play about what is relevant to themselves and their lives, dare to take risks, learn from mistakes without any fear of failure and negotiate and set their own goals and challenges.[2]

Modelling and apprenticeship

You will have heard the now infamous phrase '*Play is the child's work*', or you may have seen it in your curriculum framework documents. They are the words of Margaret Macmillan, a nineteenth-century educationalist, who fully endorsed the sentiment of the child at work being the child at play in her child development philosophies. But how many of us would like a job which includes tasks that we like, ones that we choose because they make sense to us, a job where we have an impact on the detail of what is undertaken and one where we can influence the decisions made about the tasks of the job? A job that has no autonomy or choice can lead to feeling demotivated, undervalued and unsatisfied.

That level of freedom of choice is the cornerstone in a child's most rewarding play. Play experiences of choice are unfettered by constraints, rules or prior associations. Children are often unsure of and unconcerned by the outcome or consequences in their play. Their sense of curiosity and exploration of their new world is the overwhelming feature of any and every action taken. Mari Guha worked on psychological research that established that being in control was crucial for effective learning, and this combined with choice and opportunity provides the fabric for really enriching play.[3] More recently, the Play for a Change Review for the National Children's Bureau identified the significance of play in children developing resilience and self-esteem, essential factors for their future life-long wellbeing.[4]

Put yourself in an early years setting, or indeed anywhere that young children are playing. You have devised a well-thought-out plan of activities linked by sensible differentiation for particular children. You have made available all the resources they may need and have linked the planning to the term's theme as decided at the last committee meeting or staff development day. Ask yourself, are your actions based on what you think the children would choose to do, or more importantly are they based on the observations you are aware that staff need to make on certain children since they only attend two mornings a week? Whatever the motive and however well intentioned the tasks are, your exercising control over these tasks can only have a detrimental effect on a child's motivation to engage with them. More worryingly, you are hijacking their play.

Now imagine or remember how you learnt to do the job that you do. Chances are someone was alongside you that first couple of days. No matter how menial, technical, solitary or communal, someone will have shown you or described to you how to do the job you do. You were, no matter how briefly or for how long, someone's apprentice.

The theory bit

All social constructivist theories of child development involve an idea of the child as apprentice to a mentor, facilitator or more experienced other. The understanding that a child's childhood is constructed in relation to and in response to the world around them is fundamental to these theories. Whatever the terms used, the process of the more experienced other supporting the child is the essence of what many of our modern policies and practices seek to bring to life. From Vygotsky's zone of proximal development, Bruner's play spiral model, Bowlby's attachment theory and Malaguzzi's pedagogy of listening – all recognise the child as an active agent of their own development.

The significant child development theorists that impact specifically on understanding the modern interpretations of how children learn and develop are Piaget and Vygotsky. There are many others, but these two are significant in terms of social and language development, in that they are in opposition to each other. Piaget considered that children cognitively developed from the 'inside out' and that they would pass through various and sequential stages; stages largely unaffected by the contexts and environments in which the child existed. His theory was similar to Erikson's psychosocial theories in that he too defined a sequential, and conditional, set of psychological stages that a child would pass through as it got more mature. Vygotsky, however, defined his theories on an 'outside in' view of the child: that the social and environmental context for a child's learning and development was all important.

All these understandings, or constructions, of a child's development being in relation to or response to their social environment, are all variations of a social constructivist theory.

But who shows children how to play?

On a recent Sunday morning, not unlike others since our newest child became about two years old, the noise of conflict echoed around the house. Dad had got down the wooden train track from the cupboard, had put two or three pieces together and left the room, leaving a minefield of potential angst behind him as he returned to the kitchen to finish making a cup of tea. Connor, at five years old, had a well-used favourite plan for the construction of the wooden tracking and was busy selecting his 'useful' engines. He was clear in the purpose of his play, of the track, the plan for construction, which carriage went with which loco, all decided by prior supremacy of ownership. It was his, no question. Lewis, aged two, keen to experience what this interesting addition to the things in the room would mean to him, moved into the middle and sat down on the three pieces of track Connor had just put together. So the trouble began; for every piece of track or train touched and then unattended, Lewis would pick it up, taste it, examine it, move it or discard it. Not yet able to fix it together for himself, he moved about over the constructed track, deconstructing it and sublimely oblivious to why these actions were causing distress to his older brother. Dad came back to the room to see what was going on; seeing that one child's action is interrupting the play purpose of the other, and because the older child's purpose has more perceived meaning to the adult, the younger child is withdrawn from the new things and brought into the kitchen, and this is the offensive action, the kitchen door was then shut. What follows is tears and angry upset. Not only had the new interesting things been in sight and then withdrawn, but Lewis's sense of any ownership over either the wooden track or control over events, or crucially, his imposed containment behind a closed door, felt like a punishment; it certainly sounded like one.

The overwhelming thought that occurred to me as I listened to the situation was '*Who IS going to show the younger child how to play with the track?*' Was it down to him that the older child was not active about including him in the play or showing any empathy towards him? Or that Dad moved to isolate the siblings from each other rather than take time to model a more cooperative version of the play with them both included? This new sibling was going nowhere, he was staying; and the train track, I was sure, would remain a favourite. What was needed was a new way for both the boys to engage with the track in a positive way. They both needed help to renew what it meant to them. Luckily, Connor, as the older sibling, understood that Lewis, of course, was going to be interested in the track and its possibilities, and that it was down to him and I to be the 'experts' to show Lewis how to be actively included in the current purpose, and how to play with it.

What was most noticeable was the almost immediate discontinuation of noise caused by distress, replaced with a caring '*This is how you do it, my darling*' from Connor as Lewis hunched up his shoulders in delight at being included. The lesson for me as an adult was about the need to remain alert and tuned into children as our charges. It was also a lesson about the occasional need for us all to be prepared to unlearn the patterns of what we know. This 'unpatterning' comes easier to children; maybe it is the neural plasticity of young children's brains that Fine refers to.[5] But the ability to 'unpattern' later serves to become the ability to moderate our actions in the light of new knowledge.

Love of language

As practitioners, we have a responsibility to facilitate good quality play. This is not play that necessarily makes sense to us or is of our making, but instead makes us become a willing playmate, attentive to the play purpose of the children we are engaging with. The essence of good play, as children see it, is time, ownership, agency and a means and opportunity to communicate ideas and feelings. We have a duty to model how to embrace and be playful with language. As a young child's brain becomes mature enough to begin the process of language acquisition, noises and sounds and what they represent begin to connect. This starts the process of crucial cognitive development for young children. Connecting verbal symbols to gestures and actions are often confirmed by the imitation of both. Most of us would probably, and quite unconsciously, '*wave bye bye*' to a young child as we said the words. We certainly would return the wave from a young child, imitating their action and affirming the appropriateness of both the noise and the action. Being playful with language is a habit that can provide practice, and importantly, confidence and freedom to practice for the youngest of children. This can often best be done by doing it first. I am not just talking about funny sounding words, the toilet words or made-up words. For the youngest of our children, all the words are made up! I refer more to the sequences of words that can demonstrate that a child has come to a new cognitive or relational understanding.

At the age of two and a half, going through the ritual of teeth brushing one day, the flow of water from the tap was, as ever, the focus of the conversation. Pointing animatedly, Connor gesticulated to my turning it on more. It quickly became a game of yes, no, yes.

> Mummy: '*Yes, No, Yes, No, Yes, No*'
> Connor: '*Yes, No, Yes, No, Yes*' (with an animated nod of head)
> Mummy: '*Yes, No, No, No, Yes, No*'
> Connor: '*Yes, No, Yes, Yes, Yes, Yes*' (giggles)
> Mummy: '*No, No, No, No and No*'
> Connor: '*Yes, Yes, Yes, and Yes*' (both giggling).

This sounds almost a song if you can find a tune to fit, but this is also an example of expressing choice and influencing another with words. Three years later, while I watch Connor play his Nintendo DS game of Super Mario, with alarming dexterity I fear, the same, only more sophisticatedly applied, language skill emerged. Putting the significance and influence of the consumerism and branding issues at play here aside, he uses the same cognitive skill to negotiate my choice of character.

> Connor: '*Choose one, Mummy*'
> Mummy: '*Ok, that one*' (pointing at the crocodile character to drive my virtual car 'Kart')
> Connor: '*Not that one*'
> Mummy: '*OK, which one?*'
> Connor: '*That one or that one*' (pointing at the Mario or Luigi characters)
> Mummy: '*Ok, Luigi*'
> Connor: '*No, what about Mario, Mummy?*'

The relational skill of negotiating with others and influencing others with a solid cognitive command of language is a necessary one. Often wrapped up together with an academic education or perceived to be determined by social status in the contemporary adult world, the basic skill of being able to make your preferred choice or idea understood by another is a fundamental life skill. The adults with whom children share their world need not withhold certain terms, words or phrases; instead they need to share and model how it is appropriate to use them. How many of us have not heard the word 'naughty' or 'stupid' in a childcare setting in the last ten years, except to remind new colleagues that these words are never appropriate to use. Do we remember why? How would we explain the why not to a four year old?

The holy grail of truly enriching play, and children developing an ability to be social in that play, is the harnessing of their drive to explore, imitate and model what they see and experience, with skills of engaging empathically with others. The use and value of language, particularly in the context of children's friendships, is what helps children learn to relate themselves to the world around them. Being able to enjoy talking and listening with another person is the best foundation to have for future literacy and cognitive understanding of language and its symbolic representational use in the world. To engage with children, their ideas and being able to listen to them – really listen to them, even when they don't have good command of the most correct vocabulary – can offer insights into what they are like as people.

By respecting children as a valuable part of society, regardless of age, is to give them ownership of what the world means to them. It gives them a sense of place and belonging within themselves and the things that surround them. Many practitioners will have cherished anecdotes of how children have endearingly referred to a new piece of knowledge in a way that only they could. Who would correct the child who asks '*Can you do my button belly up please?*' This innocent and harmless understanding is endearing to us, and reminds us of how simple the child's view can be.

If we can refrain from controlling their play agendas and, instead, tolerate their necessarily immature understanding of their world around them, their ownership of ideas as they see things will remain with them. As does the control for moderating those ideas as they change their mind and deepen their knowledge. Adaptation, moderation and empathy for others are all unteachable, but highly desirable in the modern, changeable world we live in.

Challenges and dilemmas

When modelling play skills with children we need to be mindful of our own need to make sense of things, as well as our adult drive to instruct them because we often know more facts. Let their own, often immature, sense of meaning occur to them with active interaction and without interference from us. It is important not to hijack their purpose and to allow children time to acknowledge their ideas and put into words what they appear to be doing. Do not redirect their choices with your adult purpose or agenda. Try this non direction, you will find it harder than you might think. But why? From a well- intentioned perspective, we want to increase their knowledge and move them to a better understanding of the world. Often, in the modern childcare context, we have a purpose for generating a visible improvement in a child's progress. But what we have often done, as unpalatable as it can be, is undermine their sense of ownership of what they were discovering.

Being unable to play with others effectively can have a debilitating impact on a child's opportunities to socialise; it can hinder their confidence in interacting with others, and can damage their developing sense of self to an extent that they might stop trying. More worryingly, they can instead develop behaviours that ultimately justify such perceived shortcomings. We all hear of the school-aged child that finds it so challenging to share that they become isolated from friendship groups, and negatively referred to by the adults around them. Unwittingly, it has possibly been our lack of care or concern earlier on that has disadvantaged the over-competitive or boastful child later in their childhood.

CHAPTER 3

Active learning; learning to be sociable

> By definition, the newborn, although evidently human, cannot yet be social, it has yet to be socialized.[1]

When we think of active learning, our first thought might be of the 'busyness' of children's actions. As early years teachers and practitioners, we may be convinced of the value of play as the most potent place for those actions to happen. We may be sure of the importance of children having first-hand experiences and plenty of support to fully embellish those experiences for each individual child. Claxton and Carr[2] introduced their ideas around children being '*ready, willing and able*' to learn, and the importance of children developing favourable dispositions for life-long learning. For me, there are three areas of particular significance when we are talking about children's social development: the physical, the emotional and the practice.

Children's physical development may not be the obvious first aspect of development we consider when thinking about how they learn to be socially adept, but to gain mastery over their own bodies is a foundation of their future self-concept, self-esteem and sense of capability and self-belief. It is the first step of their taking control. '*Children need to feel at home in their bodies and so gain mastery, and they need to be able to form relationships.*'[3]

By providing firm handling and a sensitivity of individual needs, it is possible to build strong trusting relationships. The concept that a child's having power over their physical actions strengthens their ability to make judgements, and in turn, helps nurture good self-esteem, has been explored by many.

Dweck and Leggett offered a concept of 'mastery' and 'learned helplessness' for emotional development in young children, that is, the attitudes that individuals develop about their own personal effectiveness.[4] They found that helpless children differed from mastery-orientated children in their ideas about intelligence and personality. They also described how children who had a disposition of 'learned helplessness' believe failure to be due to a lack of ability, and mastery-orientated children perceive failure to be a lack of effort, and as such, under their control.

The refraction of the secure relationship

Possibly the most vital condition for good social development for a child is a strong sense of self-esteem and self-efficacy. The development of self-esteem has its foundations in the quality of children's earliest interactions and relationships. Through the lens of a secure relationship, children can develop strong attachments and trust in others and the quality of early attachment has life-long effects on an individual's relationships with loved ones. '*The way children feel about themselves is not innate or inherited, it is learned*.'[5]

In a secure relationship with others they feel secure to practise conflict and the return to emotional balance, hypothesise and rehearse outcomes for actions and responses and to develop a secure sense of who they are in relation to their world. This 'safe place' for emotional development – one which offers respect and dignity to them, and supports the practice of their becoming emotionally resilient – underpins the blueprint for their relationships for the rest of their lives.

Allowing children to feel in control of their bodies and how they feel about themselves lays the foundations for ensuring children have a secure sense of self-esteem, believing their efforts can make a difference. This helps to ensure that their genuine choice to be sociable, rather than a lack of mastery or low self-esteem, does not affect their social development adversely. The alternative is not a life without learning, but is a life with an in-built predisposition to feel unworthy of any effort or time spent by others.

Planet Lewis

Children do not arrive with the understanding of how to communicate for the things they want, or the language to make it happen. The social nuances of how to persuade, compromise and negotiate have still to be learned along the way. The youngest of our children, who have yet to learn to sympathise, empathise or become aware that others may have needs and feelings of their own, live on their own little planet. Freud called this the Id, Piaget called it egocentrism, and Erikson saw it as Phase 2 of social and emotional development.

I want to introduce the concept of what our household calls Planet Lewis. On Planet Lewis, dealing with Lewis's agenda is far superior to any practical or sensible request made by someone else. Here, there is no one or nothing but Lewis to attend to. At just over two years old, with few words, lots of demands and a thirst for independence, life on Planet Lewis is held to ransom by the wants of Lewis.

But for Lewis to learn to be sociable in the context of his life, he needs, as does every young child, to understand how he fits into this life, and develop a self-concept and sense of identity unique to him. He needs to transform his planet into one that includes others, and their needs. This is a process called social referencing, when a child gauges their impact on the world by the reaction they receive from the adult caring for them, and the people around them. The individual person-alities of those involved have to adapt to a shifting dynamic, and most importantly, approach it with a positive, loving perspective. Children need to know that they matter, that they are valued and respected. This is fundamental to how they feel about themselves and the self-confidence they will develop.

Standing on their own two feet

The dictionary definition of 'to toddle' is an interesting one. *Collins* says that, '*As a noun it is the act or an instance of toddling, and a toddler is a child who has only just learnt to walk*'. It defines act of toddling as, '*to walk with short unsteady steps, as a child does when learning to walk*'.[6]

What it also describes is that early walking is performed with unsteady steps and at the pace of an amble or stroll. But for the modern-day toddler, life is anything but an amble. There is an almighty rush to get them to nursery, get them sleeping through the night and get them self-regulating their own emotions. This also applies to how a toddler is expected to learn to speak and learn the socially appropriate rules of the wider world. There are some allowances made for the first child in a family, since the parents are often new to parenting as the child is to life. Other than that, there can be big expectations for the child with other children around them in their family, to simply and quickly 'pick it up'. But as a culture, how long do we really let them remain 'unsteady'?

The stuff of zest

Michael Foley[7] talks of zest as the mental state of being 'in the present', the natural high of seeking out or striving for meaning, for understanding or purpose. Without the presence of recall or previous associations or expectations, the first-time experience of discovery for children is full of zest. And so it can be when children are actively learning.

As the only inhabitant of Planet Lewis, Lewis stands in the kitchen, pointing and repeating '*uh, uh, uh*'. No one responds. He comes to me at the breakfast table, reaches for my hand, taking it away from my being able to eat my own breakfast, tightly holds my forefinger and pulls on it until I get up.

> Me to Lewis: '*Oh Lew, what do you want? I am trying to eat!*'
> Lewis drags me across the kitchen and repeats the pointing and '*uh, uh, uh*'.
> Me to Lewis: '*What do you want? Do you want a drink?*'
> Lewis nods his head vigorously up and down, so I get a cup and go to the fridge.
> Me to Lewis: '*Do you want juice?*'

Again he vigorously nods his head, pats his tummy with both hands, and pads his feet in a running on the spot action. And that is when I see it. He has his eyes closed! And he is beaming a wide-opened mouth grin. His mission complete, he is delighted with himself. The reward is not just the juice, it is the command of power he has over his adult. He has found the communication route, without discernible language, to fulfil his thirst needs. His actions were motivated, auton-omous, propelled by independent desire and successful.

Play, the supporting role

Play that is open-ended, free of constraints and with no agenda other than children's own, promotes and nurtures this 'glow of living', or 'zest', that we often see in children. Elkind[8] suggests that great discoveries can be made when harmony between a child's interests, the motivation to play and opportunity to explore all converge. When the opportunities, experiences and resources for play are accompanied by a sense of ownership and agency, the crucial ingredients for transformation are present. To be willing to falter, amend meaning and purpose without distress or conflict, is 'play' in its purest form. It is their zestfulness that needs to be firstly genuinely accepted, and then, purposefully harnessed in our work with young children.

The same transformation of understanding happens with language, both verbal and non-verbal. As we become more mature language users, and we command an increasing vocabulary, we can become reliant on verbal, rather than the non-verbal methods of communication. Our non-verbal language moves into our subconscious as the 'out loud' language prevails in most of our relationships and interactions with others. The non-verbal becomes resigned to our more intimate social moments, when we seek the comfort, approval and guidance through the subtle nuances of movements, sounds and behaviours in others. The significance and enabling place of non-verbal language in effective and social interactions and communications with young children cannot be underplayed.

Non-verbal communication

For very young children using pre-linguistic language, the signals and messages our bodies and movements convey are the main source of our communication with them. They very quickly come to understand that a flat hand or pointed forefinger towards their head, often coupled with the sounds that accompany it, means 'No'. This refusal then becomes the trigger for a strong behaviour response from them.

We eventually move the non-verbal communication we rely on as infants to a bottom drawer of social skills as we mature to become competent language users. But the significance of that early language is not lost; it is there. It remains, but becomes subconscious. Have you ever had the content of an electronic message or text misunderstood? It is the lack of non-verbal communication in the electronic medium, and the lack of voice intonation that speaking offers us to support the bare words, that can lead to such misunderstanding. The same applies to our understanding each other, when one has a good command of language and the other does not.

Reading the signals and patterns of play

Have you ever witnessed the child at play who carefully, and repeatedly, places the small-world animals around the edge of the table, or around the edge of the small-world farm activity on offer? Have you then seen this same child sit for lunch and line his packed lunch box contents around the edge of his plate? These events are completely unrelated: one is called free play, a time of choice for the child to engage with his own interests; the other is lunchtime, a functional or social time scheduled in to a timetable as an essential Ofsted requirement. However the schema on show is the same, and the child is threading its understanding of how objects can be positioned around the edge or boundaries of things; this is known as a radial schema. This child's active learning transcends the curriculum, the schedule, the timetable and the adult agenda. Being able to recognise these patterns of play can be mightily useful when reading the signals of where children are cognitively. It was Chris Athey's work at the Froebel Nursery Research Project in the 1970s, based on Piaget's early concepts of schemas, that first defined a set of schemas or patterns of behaviour which children actively employ to explore the world around them. If you are aware of the transporting schema, for example, it can help to make sense and connect the actions of the child who has spent all day putting seemingly unrelated things inside vehicles to then move them to another place. The child who throws almost everything and has her behaviour negatively referred to as 'just a phase', might instead be just playing out a trajectory schema. The adult should resist stopping it and, instead, offer tolerable limits to what things can be thrown and where. Often, children's actions can be a combination of a number of schemas, such as the child who posts everything that comes through the letterbox under the cooker; this action is just the positioning, trajectory and enclosure schemas at play. We all have habits and patterns of behaviour that are formed based on our early schematic experiments. Do you know anyone that always has to straighten their desk, plate and cutlery, shelves or objects in a particular way? Or someone who never doodles in straight lines? Or has a liking for boxes? We all know of one, not necessarily someone whose life is inhibited by habits or compulsive tendencies. We are all comforted by certain rituals, habits and patterns of behaviour.

Behaviour stakes

It is our adult need to connect and categorise events and actions which drives us to label and assess the child's phase, stage, behaviour or current schema. This is particularly true in current educational environments when we are dealing with behaviour management. There is an approach which says, 'If we can label it, we can have a strategy to deal with it'. The management of behaviour has become such a beast in its own right that we have begun to employ 'behaviour management' specialists, learning mentors and 'behaviour buddies' in schools to work with those children that have perceived behavioural issues. We are coached to separate the inappropriate behaviour from the person doing it so as not to label that child, damage their self-esteem, or undermine their developing sense of worth. Current fashionable practice includes specific reward and punishment strategies, empowering individuals to take personal responsibility and recognise for themselves what might be inappropriate behaviour and its consequences. Strategies vary, from withdrawing the biting infant from an incident in a way to allow them to see the bitten victim receive positive, caring attention and sympathy for their injury, to the controversial 'mars bar' culture that is offered to excluded young teens in attempts to re-engage with them. All have a category, label, assessment process or policy strategy to help adults to deal with it.

Often for the child, there is no understanding that the way they are behaving is difficult, disruptive or upsetting to others; they are too busy experiencing it to witness it. It is only as children get older that being asked to reflect on their behaviour is effective in addressing the consequences of their actions. In our fast moving culture, who makes time to really do this with children?

Learning to self-regulate emotions

Learning to regulate their own emotions is a crucial element in a child's social development. This control the child has of their emotional responses allows them to be the master of the impact their social experiences have on their relationships. The blueprint of how they will deal with sadness, anger, doubt, happiness, elation, pride and jealousy throughout their lives begins in these early years. For really young children who are still learning to manage and regulate their emotions they can understandably become overwhelmed with their emotions to an extent that means they are unable to come back to 'normal' by themselves. Gerhardt describes '*a dance of mutual responsiveness*' between child and carer as they practise how to manage difficult emotions. She also eloquently elaborates how, if feelings are modelled as useful guides to the inner states of others, as well as to your own, and respectfully responded to, then a '*culture arises in which other's feelings matter, and you are motivated to respond*'.[9] Learning to self-regulate is a tricky business and can be exhausting for the child and the adult involved. As practitioners, we grow an awareness of the child's feeling state, and subconsciously tune into 'where they are at'. Emotional distress and the noises that come with it are distinct and can mean a child is struggling to come back to an emotional 'normal' by themselves.

If a child is on a cycle of emotion that requires help from another to bring them back to normal, often the most effective way is not to attempt to reason with the child, but instead to interrupt the course of emotions. Let me explain. When, on a three-hour train journey, I made my way to the buffet car for a coffee, I passed a young father trying to console a small child, who was crying hysterically in the compartment between the carriages. I offered him a sympathetic look and an 'it can be so hard travelling with little ones' and carried on. I passed mum in the next carriage, who was gesturing to dad that she come and take over, concerned for the public disruption that her child was causing, second only to the small boy's distress. On my way back, they had swapped places; she was sitting by the carriage door, red faced and visibly struggling with his upset, as he cried into a frenzy. I stopped to ask if she was ok and would she like a 'shot of caffeine' for her nerves. She smiled. I crouched in front of her and began, with the softest voice I could manage on the busy carriage, to ask her where they were travelling to and lament with her how hard I had found it to travel with my own small children. After a couple of minutes, the small boy sniffed and sobbed more quietly, as he looked at me to strain to hear my words. At this point, I began to rub his little socked foot as he stretched his hand to his mum's cleavage. She apologised for his seeking this particular comfort and we joked of how he would probably never grow out of that. We talked a little more, and it was only as the boy began to snore that we talked of how sometimes just remembering to change pace is important. By distracting mum enough to calm her a little, her son was interrupted in his objection to every-thing, which was enough to calm him too. He had forgotten why he had started crying at all. My interruption was enough to calm them both and possibly even transform the potential pattern of behaviour that this intense emotional experience might prompt in the future for either or both of them.

Transformation of understanding

Loris Malaguzzi was the Italian early education specialist who was also the founder of the preschool phenomenon in Reggio Emilia in Northern Italy whose philosophy is often referred to as the Reggio approach, He described the drive to transform understanding and reconstruct it, as a process of *'continual reconstruction of their (children's) identity'*.[10] He believed that central to the philosophy was an uncompromising image of the child as being full of wonder and curiosity, and capable of co-constructing his or her own knowledge. He also highlighted the increased potency of this reconstruction of understanding when it occurs through interactions with others, and within significant relationships.

The ability to transform our understanding and reconcile the new with what we knew before is crucial in becoming socially and emotionally competent in relationships and being able to relate and empathise with others. To do this we need to become practised at how to be unbalanced in intimate social exchange, and how to respond to that in order to bring ourselves, and our relationship with our new reconstruction of ourselves, back to comfort. *'It is a desire to reformulate a more balanced situation that allows you to have relationships'*.[11]

If we were to name this process as 'conflict', we might jump to the adult associa-tions and meanings the term holds for us, but conflict is not always a negative thing. Unresolved conflict, that becomes angry and confrontational, is. Children need time, space and opportunity to practice how to respond to social and emotional imbalance, and unfettered play together with loving adults offer these things. The value of social play and uninterrupted time to experiment with the social dynamics that children come across is essential.

Social intimacy

Intimacy is the sister, daughter and mother of social relationships, language and social development. The capacity for forming and maintaining intimacy is learnt from the earliest relationships a child experiences. Bowlby, Gerhardt, Kaplan and Chodorow all describe and explore the importance of a smooth transition to separateness without losing the capability to empathise and be socially intimate with others. In particular, when referring to really young children, Sue Gerhardt's view on the process of weaning children off the intimate love between the key care-giver and the young child, which helps them begin to self-regulate their surging emotions, offers a clear explanation of a crucial, yet intangible and immeasurable element in a child's social development. This is the need for children to intrinsically feel valued enough to know that they have a safe place for emotional comfort, should they want it. Malaguzzi believed that the most indispensable feature of working with children is developing a personal relationship with each child, a relationship that is based on respect and values the child as *rich in potential, strong, powerful and competent*.[12] The child is recognised as having his or her own values, as someone who wants to be respected and valued for themselves as well as holding respect for others and who embodies a curiosity and open-mindedness to all that is possible.

Pace and rhythm

There are many parents and practitioners who endorse the value of routine in children's lives. It provides points of reference for children about the sequence of events that occur in daily life. From a child's earliest days, the routine of feeding, sleeping, playing and quiet time can help to establish constancy and consistency for the developing child. Routine offers a rhythm to the order of life. The fast moving world in which many western families live is full of commotion and can be dismissive of the value of stillness and solitude. But the quiet time to reflect, recall and ruminate is crucial for children learning to relate to their world, and transforming their emotional state to cope with the new version as new experiences and feelings influence them.

There is a new phenomenon of social diseases that our youngest children will maybe have to learn to live with such as a lack of sufficient sleep, inadequate diets, minimal exercise, increased pollution, paranoid parenting, over stimulation due to digital technologies and growing up unrealistically risk averse.

All these may become true for many children, but if we can slow the pace that they are raced through childhood and offer pauses to their lives for them to ruminate, speculate and, most importantly, daydream, it can help to stabilise experiences of what will become their memories of the future. For early years teachers and practitioners who are often constrained by the obligations of the frameworks in which they have to operate, it is important to remember that there has yet to be government legislation for what can be said between people. As we know how important high quality interactions within secure relationships are to babies and young children and their social development, then it is a prime task for us to ensure that there is always quality time, opportunity and space to respectfully interact with others, and in turn, model to children how to do it for themselves.

Challenges and dilemmas: for whom are the 'terrible twos' terrible?

This use of the phrase 'terrible twos' has, for a long time, bothered me as both a practitioner and parent. It assumes a negative stage through which most children need to pass. I raise it now because the young child's early flexing of its 'free will muscles' can have implications for future behavioural patterns and is so very often referred to negatively. The toddler years see a shift in focus from the biological to the social. With their infancy still a strong memory, their child is contrary, having tantrums and has discovered that having opinions gets results. Have you ever heard a toddler, shout 'NO', whilst using their new found physical strength to pull away from you? Wild horses can be easier to manage.

I want, instead, to suggest that it is a period of time that is often more of a challenge for adults. Could it be that it is our insensitivity to a child's subtle change of their learning lens on their experiences that causes many of the conflicts?

The social meal

Consider the two-year-old child that used to be a better eater, but is now less interested in food, more easily distracted by the noise and commotion around and more wilful, it seems to us, not to conform at mealtimes. This age and the behaviours that are, in our culture, associated with this age can make their struggle for independence exasperating for us as practitioners and parents. But reflect a moment: what are we actually offering this child as they sit to eat? Is it primarily a nutritious meal, time to refuel, or a valuable social experience?

This now more cognitively mature child has learned to trust that its basic biological needs will be met and that it can expect to be fed or can get its hunger signals responded to; what the child craves now is the social meal. We, as adults, have long established patterns about food: some of us have our comfort foods, our treat foods, our bad habits with food. The youngster's newest agenda is the social experience it has learned can come with food. It is us that remains focused on the vital task of nourishing them in the literal sense long after it needs to be, rather than recognising the child's renewed appetite for all things social. If the social experience you offer alongside the food is not as engaging as the social 'stuff' going on behind you, dinner will most definitely be over, this time.

Good for a change

Dr Richard Restak, in his book *The New Brain*, describes the plasticity of the human brain as the brain's capacity for change.[13] The brain is transforming itself

Figure 3.1 *The social meal*

all the time in response to the experiences we have, throughout a human's life. The newness of a child's brain, and the speed with which it develops new neural pathways and undergoes synaptic pruning, could maybe provide some reason for the 'terrible twos' as a 'stage of conflict'.

Maybe we just can't keep up with them!

CHAPTER 4

Creating sociable language

Adults assume that the reason friendship develops is that people like one another. Children, in contrast, see proximity, or being with someone, the first and basic element of friendship.[1]

Being sociable involves a lot of emotional energy. It requires an investment of the senses, the use of memory and recall, as well as the conscious, active engagement with another person. As adults we have, whether we are aware of it or not, a duty to model how to be a competent social being in the world in which we live both to our children and the children that we might be responsible for. As parents and practitioners, we should be acutely aware of the need for our children to become adept at being socially acceptable to their peers and the wider world around them. We are crucially placed to provide them with opportunities to see, practise and discover what sociable language and behaviour looks and feels like.

Permission to practice

I want to draw attention to the practise of practice. As children, the most important purpose of practising language and being sociable is to learn that it is perfectly acceptable to be playful with words and language and there is no getting it wrong – only misjudging the context in which the language is used. Let me explain what I mean.

When working in a local nursery recently, I was enjoying some reading time with a group of boys and girls. We were loosely following the story by the pictures, the contexts of what the characters were doing and making songs about the noises they may have been making. With lots of '*whooing-whooing*' and '*nee-nawing*', we were beautifully lost in the pages of a colourful and engaging book. It was not long, however, before one of the children offered the suggestion of '*poo-poo*' and then '*wee-wee*' as names for the characters in our story. Some of the other children giggled and covered their mouths, darting their eyes from the maverick name giver and me and back, awaiting my reaction. Brilliant, I said, '*but what rhymes with poo?*' We all were giggling as we tried sounds that sounded like poo and which suited our story telling. With a quick '*and she wears great big shoe, shoes!*' we continued. It was at this point that just as we were singing our new rhyme with our new words, '*poo-poo*' and '*that's just what we do-do*', another adult came into the room. This adult interjected a stern '*No thank you!*' from the other side of the room.

The adult was judging how appropriate these words were without registering the social and language contexts we were using them in. She was using her own learned social etiquette rules and values about what language is socially appropriate. What this very experienced practitioner did for the children, however, was to emphasise how not using the 'right' or 'socially correct' words can be more important than experimenting with the ideas and language creativity our curious brains would like to use them for. She was also not in the room at the time we began the story-telling and so was unable to put our rhyme into context.

No wonder children favour such words in the first place. For them, it must be very tantalising to evoke the reaction of adults by using, and misusing, these words. And that is the point: it the reaction and response of those around them that provides them with understanding about social and language contexts and rules. Even very young children can competently misuse language to excite a response in adults; it could even be argued that they actively seek to do this.

The context of conversation

It could be argued that young children have a heightened interest in the responses of those around them, as they begin to understand how the social world works. This same interest motivates the acquiring of communication. Early communication begins with observation and becomes first an imitation of what they see and hear. This then becomes a child's learned response, or pattern of reaction, to actions they perceive. This linear process happens both in terms of social behaviour and to both body and verbal language. Schaffer describes this inevitable process as social referencing, a process that every human being goes through.[2]

What the words mean

For infants and very young pre-linguistic children, the repetitive use of vocabulary, often accompanied by gesture or action to reinforce its intended meaning, helps to provide symbolic representation of what a word means.

Vygotsky defined this process as *internalisation*, an internally understood response to an outside process or sequence experienced; a process of repeated action and reaction which then embeds expectation. Connolly eloquently offers an example of an infant child pointing to demonstrate it.

> At first, an infant's movement represents little more than a failed attempt to grasp an object outside of their reach. Their arm remains outstretched and orientated towards that object. However, it is when an adult responds to the child's movements that the situation changes. The infant's attempts to grasp the object tend to be interpreted by those around them as a gesture and lead them

to fetch the object for the infant. Over time the infant begins to reinterpret their behaviour in light of the interpretations and activities of those around them. Thus, what began as an unsuccessful attempt to grasp an object comes to be understood and used by the infant as a gesture actually directed at another person.[3]

This action and response internalisation process is the same for children learning to use the appropriate language responses to certain interactions and situations in the culture in which they live. Culturally appropriate language is socially created, absorbed by children and endorsed, or not, by our response to it.

When introducing a child to swimming for the first time, by using a repeated sequence of words and actions, a child who may have lost the naturalistic, innate response to being immersed in water by holding their breath can be reprogrammed to do so. By saying the child's name to gather their individual attention, using the word 'ready' to warn them of what is coming next, and then the action of submerging them under the water can, with repetition, prompt them to breathe in during submersion.

For older, talking children, activities and opportunities that offer to enhance their willingness to attempt communication and encourage the practice of vocabulary are crucial. The use of open-ended resources such as natural resources, boxes, water, light, cushions etc., resources that have no particular outcome but provide limitless opportunity to explore their ideas, can support children's imaginative and creative tendencies. Anything that can prompt representational thinking for young children, offer them possibilities to recreate things and experiences, try things out or develop new ideas, can heighten a young child's ability to use new language. They can transcend the social difficulties that new social encounters sometimes present them with. The development of their ability to symbolically represent things, ideas and thoughts with language enhances their cognitive processes. Their drive and confidence to attempt to vocalise what they see and hear, and with an increasing competence in language and vocabulary, their motivation to express their thoughts and ideas bubbles up and out of them.

The chitter, chatter of children

It is not just the physical and cognitive changes that occur in a child's early years that are critical. Social contact with adults and peers is equally, if not more, important.[4]

Friendships provide a particularly important foundation for young children in which to explore new experiences. Shared experiences in adult free spaces provide valuable freedom for ideas, creativity and new language. The words children use between them, the playful alternatives they invent and the codes they develop to shut us out are all part of the freedom we should allow them, as they practise symbolically representing their ideas with each other. I will explore the value and importance of peers and early friendships later in Chapters 5 and 9.

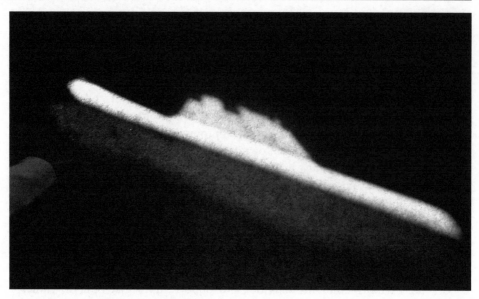

Figure 4.1 *Look at the sunshine boat!*

The context of conversation

There is evidence that children with more opportunities to engage in social encounters, either from larger families[5] or with siblings and adult relatives,[6] have a more rapid development of a representational theory of mind. Helen Bee says that '*When young children play together, they expand each other's experience with objects and suggest new ways of pretending to one another, thus fostering still further cognitive growth*'.[7]

Having a representational theory of mind means being able to think of things in an abstract sense, without a tangible, visible representation of what it means. It heightens a child's ability to think about concepts, and crucially, to think creatively and critically. It gives them awareness of there being other ways of being, playing and thinking. This in turn frees them to play with 'what ifs' and often coincides with a vocabulary explosion, as they seek to express new thinking and corroborate with others to play out those ideas.

During a term of 'All about me' themed activities, birthdays, ages and heights were all new concepts to two of the young boys. Their new connected thinking produced a clash of concepts and was symbolically and confidently represented as follows:

> Child A to me: '*But I should go first because I am five months taller than him! He is 4 and I am 5!*'
>
> Child B to Child A: '*But Feberry (February) is before May! I should go first!*'

Finding the funny

A life-long love of language can be encouraged when young children have permission and the opportunity to be playful with it. From playing Peekaboo to subversive noise making and deliberate use of adult shockers, children love to find the words that prompt adults to interact, and in particular, to be playful with them. One of the key attributes of the effective practitioner is the ability to be comfortable as the playmate of the young child, who has the ability to be playful on their terms, and is proficient at being playful with language. This is to encourage children to know that there are no wrong words, only ones that are more suitable or culturally acceptable.

The theory bit

There is a strong link between secure attachment and a more rapid shift to representational theory of mind for children. When young children are emotionally secure enough to believe that they are worth interacting with, they are more intrinsically motivated to find a shared understanding of meaning with others. This hints at the importance of the quality of the social interactions children experience, as well as the quantity. Vygotsky suggested that social interactions are the arena where much of a child's cognitive growth occurs. Schaffer and Sylva and Lunt described joint involvement episodes (JIE) as a critical opportunity to develop the social framework against which quality cognitive and emotional growth take place. These JIE are intentional engagements by carer and baby, borne out of physical closeness and where both are mutually involved with each other only. Zeedyk called these '*the moments of falling in love with each other*',[8] that an attached pairing of mother and child experience together. Sylva went on to develop the educational concept of '*sustained shared thinking*' as part of the EPPE project, a practice model for high quality interaction with our youngest children.[9] Ferre Laever's Wellbeing and Involvement Scales also clearly linked a child's established sense of security with a willingness to engage with the social, cognitive and emotional world around them. Known as the Leuven Scales, they focus on identifying a child's level of engagement at what they are involved with as a direct reflection of their state of wellbeing: a learner happy to engage with learning. The levels can snapshot a child's body language and behaviours to identify any factors that may be hindering a child's capacity to explore, discover and play. Importantly, such a snapshot is undertaken within the context of a trusted, secure relationship with a known adult. This is intended to limit the variables of social and emotional stress that a new situation or person can temporarily bring to a child's sense of wellbeing.

The skills of sociable play

Have you ever worked with a child who does not yet know how to play sociably? It is not any particular signal that gives the game away; instead it is the lack of a set of skills the child has yet to learn. It is the child who has not yet demonstrated an ability or willingness to initiate play involvement with another person, either a child or an adult. Alternatively it is the child who has not yet gained the language, or the confidence to use language, to allow them access to that involvement with others. These children often watch others' actions from the sidelines, wary of a new group and can become distressed as the play moves away from their understanding or location. These children can often be found staying close to the sandpit and water table, both known as the singles bar of any childcare setting. For the child who needs to consolidate their social skills to use a particular play state free from unwanted or unknown involvement with others, the shape and size of both these activities provides a useful vantage point for the nervous child and offers a natural physical barrier. The relational play states[10] I refer to are solitary play, spectator play, parallel play, associative play and cooperative play. Before young children have sufficient social and cognitive skills that allow them to move in and out of the different modes of play, they have an initial linear development through the different states. For example, when a child feels independently and consistently able to cope with the possibility of social interaction with new others, they move from spectator to parallel play. Once comfortable with playing alongside another, they begin to move into associative play modes, where they can freely interact with others, often building play plans together with those others.

Other signs of a child unsure of how to break into a social space may be an unwillingness to engage with other, more talkative children in anything other than closed outcome activities, or a pronounced lack of negotiation ability, either using actions or words. It might be the child that wants to engage but is frustrated by the interruption of others wanting to interact with them or the child that repeatedly overreacts to a change of purpose in play. I am keenly aware of my use of the term 'stage' when referring to these types of play and would normally find another way to phrase it. Here I use it to highlight a common, but often unnoticed, frequent occurrence in early years practice. We refer to and record these 'stages' as though they were hierarchical, that one stage follows another, never to be returned to. Our preoccupation to do so belies the 'progress and outcome' educational culture we currently work in.

The social skills required for any relational play are fundamental and complementary – anything but a straight progression. A child does not move from being solitary in their play, to parallel and then to associative and on to cooperative; instead they acquire more and more skills that allow them choice about how they want to interact with others – or not. You may find solitary players residing in the better vantage points of a setting, but also the parallel players will return to find space to reconcile a new social skill they may have encountered, or find time to ruminate on a new experience or encounter, alone or with others. When children can relate associatively and cooperatively, they do not stop enjoying one-to-one contact with others or being alone. Just because I like to work in the garden with family, potting up the plants in the spring, does not mean I do not enjoy a quiet moment alone with my Alan Titchmarsh book.

Key social language skills

Collaboration and negotiation are key attributes to being competently sociable. In the same way that speaking and listening are the foundations of later literacy skills, working with others and corroborating ideas and sharing purposes are the bedrock of effective social skills.

In Chapter 2 we discussed how the purest ingredients of play are exploration and discovery, and how not hijacking a child's intended purpose with our own, often well-intentioned agenda, is vital. This is particularly relevant to this chapter's discussion of creating sociable language. Early interactions portray to children what we think of them, demonstrate to them how they can expect to be treated as children by adults, and possibly set early patterns of how they relate to others, both younger and older than them, for their whole lives.

Colwyn Trevarthen defined the intimate early communications between infant and mother as crucial in the development of a child's cognitive expectation about how to communicate with another human being.[11] 'Motherese' is the language of this close relationship and includes any part of the reciprocal process of interacting with any very young child, especially pre-linguistic children. There is strong evidence of a correlation between positive relationship habits, which are supported by high quality interactions with interested and nurturing adults early in life, and secure emotional foundations for the rest of life. It is not rocket science; I know that I soon stop seeking interactions with people that leave me feeling emotionally unsure without reason or just make me feel bad.

As the social world of the child widens, and the child learns to interact with many other different characters, both peers and adults, there can be no guarantees that they will all be positive experiences. The idea of keeping them 'safe' from characters and situations that cause difficulties or distress is felt keenly by parents and can be challenging for practitioners also. The concept of the 'curling parent' or 'hover mum' is the parent or adult that seeks to 'smooth' the way for their child, sometimes to the child's detriment. Children need to develop the social skills that help them exist harmoniously, and independently, with all types of people. When adults model a positive approach to new things and new social situations, it provides a scaffold for children's early social skills. This means being flexible, adaptable, creative and yet stable. By always ensuring that one element of a new experience is recognisable, be it you as the constant companion, a favourite resource or familiar place or story, most young children can embrace any new experience with zest.

Early habits of competent social skills can be established by encouraging a willingness in children to remain open to social opportunities and possibilities, and seek not always to be 'first', 'best' or 'right', but instead to be fair and considerate towards others. In childcare practice and youth groups, this is often supported by clear rules of play or behaviour, or ground rules of how we all like to be treated. Adults offering clear models of what are appropriate social interactions to children, both with them and with other adults, can provide a structure for emerging personalities and new social encounters, and provide subliminal clues to children about how they can effectively negotiate their own way socially with others.

The language of listening

With well-documented significance placed on the connection between a person's early wellbeing and emotional self, and the impact it has on a person's later social competency, I was reminded of a small research project by a husband and wife team.[12] They had simply observed adults talking to children. Not in nurseries or schools, or places where adults are expected to be actively involved with the formal education of children, but in their busy high street on a Saturday afternoon. Enthralled by their stark findings, I decided I needed to experience it for myself. I went to my local supermarket, took a walk down my local high street, visited a fast food outlet and spent some time in a well-known chain store.

Fundamental skills of language include listening, turn taking, reading non-verbal-signals and body language, as well as the mechanical elements such as vocabulary and grammar. What Quinn and Quinn discovered, and what my time in these surroundings showed, was a shocking lack of respect shown by the adults in their day to day interactions with children. With examples of interactions being punitive, instructional, rushed and impatiently handled by adults, there was little positive body language used to temper the negative effect of the messages being given by adults to children. Often adults spoke to children just behind them, down from their gaze either in buggies or whilst being herded along by the hand. There was little eye contact sought, no mimicry of body stance or gesture to portray an interest in any interaction with them, and when they did have control of the inter-action with the child there was a remarkable amount of finger wagging in small faces. And yet complaints abound from adults about how children don't listen, engage or pay attention. Are we sure we give them a positive reason to?

Beneath the practical aspects and conditions for effective communication, and against a backdrop of the widely acknowledged value of respectful, responsive and caring interactions, there are some less obvious skills of listening that are crucial to children's future sociability. As adults, do we take enough time to really discover another person's meaning though listening? Can we do it without irritation or impatience? How do we engage with the skill of really listening to children? And are we aware of exactly what we do? All these personal aspects of listening are habits we have developed during our lives, but how do we demonstrate to children how to listen?

Doing their talking for them

It is fashionable to agree that children have rights, deserve a voice and to be heard. Some would complain the contemporary child has too much say so and too much to say. Hugh Cunningham reminds us of a nostalgic age of 'adult solidarity', when boundaries were set by adults and upheld unanimously by all other adults, or so it seemed.[13] Furedi, Palmer and Gill have all described a more recent cultural shift to risk-averse attitudes towards children and their childhoods. These societal behaviours that some adults have developed are exhausting to maintain and debilitating for both children and adults. You only have to hear of snowballs being banned on the school playground after winter's first snowfall, or full protection gear for knees and elbows before a short slope can be enjoyed, to wonder where the common sense has gone. The idea that children can judge their own risk and challenge seems to be unthinkable for many adults. The 'nanny knee' syndrome, as I like to call it, is the adult's sharp intake of breath accompanied by an 'ouuuhh' sound after a child has fallen over. At what point do we let the child decide if it hurts and decide for themselves if they need to cry out in pain? The same can be said of how we talk for children a long time after they can speak for themselves.

For our youngest children, we seek to be the ambassadors of their interests, the keepers of their wellbeing and we regularly discuss children and their needs, as is right so to do. But when do we deem children able to verbally represent themselves? Is it when they can tell us what they want or when they tell us that what they want is what we want? Or is it when they have the language and/or the appropriate social skills to present an idea or concept?

Back to the swimming pool to explain. In a busy foyer, whilst several early primary aged children were in their lesson, one parent decided to loudly complain that her child's class were doing a lot of waiting and 'mucking' about, whilst the instructor was helping two slightly less able children adjust their floats. The parent explained how this was not an isolated incident and their child was not getting anything out of the lesson. Had this parent asked their child how they found the lesson? Had they considered asking whether the child felt they were doing too much or too little or waiting around too much during their lesson? Did they think they were improving at all? Crucially, was the child enjoying chatting with their friends whilst involved with a group activity? Surprisingly young children can express a like or dislike. Possibly the issue was whether or not the child's swimming lesson was offering the value for money the parent wanted. I wondered whether anything that the parent was saying on behalf of the child had come from what the child thought.

This story is about respect, not the current youth culture version of 'respect'; instead it is about allowing and valuing another's input into decisions that affect them. Of course, I am not suggesting small child revolutionaries should take to the streets to demand spaghetti hoops for lunch every day, or that the decisions the family considers about the way their home is organised should be unrealistically determined by the youngsters in it.

Challenges and dilemmas

Having thought about the concept of becoming sociable and acquiring the language that can help children both enjoy and master the process, just give a thought to the other child. What about the child who appears self-contained and self-assured enough not to need, maybe not even enjoy, being overtly sociable? What language do we choose to describe them? Shy? Quiet? Loner? Reserved? What about the child who seems immune to the excitement that a group of young children can generate when everyone else is engaged with an activity and each other. A free spirit? A daydreamer? Many of these are seen as being detrimental to a child's learning in a school context. How well do we differentiate for them?

The other end of the scale is the child who is overtly sociable, cocky, popular with peers, but maybe 'challenging' for the adults. Any child not in the 'safe zone of sociable' (see Chapter 7) is often negatively referred to by the adult world around them. No wonder there is such a perceived crisis in childhood neuroses.

On a practical level, maybe the more sociable alternative of the backward facing buggy, the one that faces the pusher, can provide an intimate and protective social bubble for the youngest of children as they explore the world together with their significant other.

With mindful attention of how we use current safety restraints for our children, we could acknowledge the child's right to perpetual access to another human and the interactions that are so crucial for them in these earliest of years. Do we register how long the child remains in a high chair? In the back seat of a car, strapped in? As our children get older, these restraints can become more entrapping for them, reducing their freedom of movement and sense of autonomy. No wonder they can become times for conflict. Would you like to be strapped into a buggy when you have made it clear you would rather walk and take time to explore things on the journey? The destination is only important to the adult; the young child has no concept of event sequence and of 'a means to an end' – for them there is no end to the exploration available along the way.

CHAPTER 5

Seeing children talk

'Mummy, did God save our gracious Queen and how did he do it?'

Emily, aged five years

As children's own internal language rules develop, described by Chomsky as the language acquisition device, children need rich, connected first-hand experiences to practise and explore how the vocabulary and structures of the language they are learning are linked together in order to successfully convey meaning. During a routine observation some years ago, I was playing alongside a child digging out toys in the sandpit. When he dug out the small sieve, I asked, '*What have you found?*' The child answered '*A little net*'. Three times I called it a sieve, but rather than register the change of name to what I called it, the child insisted on calling it a net, using his word saying, '*This is what I am doing with the little net, I am putting all the sticky sand in the little net and then in my bucket. Then I am putting more in the little net and making a big one in the bucket. See, I shake it like this.*'

This child knew his object to be a little net and felt confident enough to want to show me that its functions suited all his needs. Thus he had become responsible for what he had learned so far about the net and what it did. My repeated reference to it as a sieve, as it may be used for cooking, was not the way this child had encountered this object in his life experience so far.

It was what he did next that remains with me. Unable to join him in his understanding of what the little net was called and what it did, he physically moved away from me! He had tried to socialise with me, find common ground with me and had even answered my pointless question about what he had found. He had tried to help me join in by explaining what he was doing. But I did not listen to him; instead my focus on progressing his understanding overcame my taking time to discover with him. This resulted in his polite dismissal of me as a playmate. I had learned a very valuable lesson that day: you must listen to children.

The safe zone of sociable

In Chapters 3 and 4 we explored how the emerging ability of children to represent things symbolically through language is supported by their having quality relationships and social interactions with those around them. There is a raft of evidence suggesting how practice, opportunity and endorsement by caring others are crucial in underpinning a child's communication skills and their potential for social development. But do we get the conditions of safe sociable environments right for our children? Do we provide the right conditions for plenty of pretend play, encourage the right states of mind, provide respectful and appropriate models of social rules, and allow enough time for their imaginations to flourish? Answering these questions could help us to define our practice in our work with young children in a way that offers the most conducive environments for rich, engaging and exploratory language opportunities.

The face value of friendships

As well as listening to children, and actively engaging with their ideas and hypotheses of how the world fits together, we need to allow them opportunities to develop shared meanings together with their peers.

Figure 5.1 *Signing and saying 'Peas'*

Their world is a shared one, where early allegiances can help them come together with ideas, construct shared meanings and begin to behave cooperatively with other people.

Sharing experiences allows children to connect together what they see, hear and experience. By grouping together, they not only have opportunity to develop friendships and discover and practise group dynamics, but can share what they understand individually with others. As they do so, they begin to understand how things are connected together, and the language used to describe it, and they are beginning to internalise their own learning and understanding in a wider context. This sharing practice encourages autonomy and self-efficacy, trust in others and, importantly, tolerance of their ideas.

As adults, we presume the closest of friendships to be based on shared experiences, memories and values. As adults we maybe have friends we made as children, went to school or college with, or have shared experiences of starting new jobs or clubs together, or becoming parents at similar times. The contexts of the friendships we have as adults changes as our own experiences change us, but for young children without the luxury of experience, their view of friendship is at face value. Children are unaware of the complexities and subtleties of adult roles and relationships before they are fully socialised. They have not yet had sufficient experience to competently and consistently apply social rules to their social interactions.

As an example, a young child who has had a toy repeatedly snatched from them by the same child will still persist with playing with that child. They do not have the emotional or language maturity to reconcile the other child's envy of their possession of the toy, nor do they have the empathic skills to want to improve the outcome of the interaction for the other child based on understanding how they feel. Only after practising sharing and experience do children learn strategies and the language to deal with snatchers, and understand that snatching from others is not socially acceptable behaviour. While children remain socially inexperienced, anyone that plays, or practises snatching, with you is qualification enough for friendship.

Mutual respect with all others is assumed by the child, since they are, as yet, unaware of the adult supremacy over children since they have no concept of 'the generalised other'. Young children are still establishing a view of themselves in relation to others and the 'other person's' viewpoint or stance is not yet perceivable. Put simply they are blissfully unaware of the natural pecking order to social status that adulthood brings, and mutual respect for all others is not questioned. It is only as they become aware of the differences between themselves and others that the cultural values and expectations of social class and status begin to influence their early perception of personal identity.

Child-to-child interactions are characterised by equality, with reciprocity and willingness to engage with the ideas of others the most prominent feature. The child-to-child world is neither real nor fantasy; they don't have enough experience to place it in one or the other, so it exists with the simple agenda of exploring possibilities together – possibilities of thinking, creating, language and practice in social and emotional resilience, skills that will underwrite all of a child's relationships throughout their lives.

Social objects

Very young children will talk to objects; they will wave bye-bye to trees, cars and buses and will attempt conversation with anything that has a face on it. They have an early grasp of the social concept that arriving requires a hello and leaving requires a bye-bye, but they do not yet understand that water leaving the bath via the plughole is not something that requires the same bye-bye as a human leaver may expect. They are not yet cognitively or socially equipped to know that objects are just and only that. But there is also the object that takes on a persona and has a prized place of sentiment for the child. The well-loved, dog-eared soft toy. You know the one, the one that you have to wait until the child is asleep before putting it through a much needed wash cycle. These security or comfort objects come in many different guises, maybe nanny's left-behind scarf, maybe a favourite label on a pillowcase. Or for Luca, an array of neck fobs and, what his mum called, pocket fillers, that he would fastidiously fill his clothes with every day. He had begun to refer to them by name and her mother was concerned it may hint at his suffering from obsessive-compulsive disorder or stress. But when you really listened to Luca explain the names for all the fobs, tags, badges and pens he cherished, you began to realise that he was not a chronically stressed four year old, but simply a boy who was carrying all his memories with him.

The practice of pretending

As the child's social development matures, the use of these trusted objects in pretend play can provide a social companion for the child as they explore possibilities imaginatively. The child who likes to chatter through the bathing of her favourite doll, or the boy who uses his watch in a 'walkie talkie' adventure, are both children with busy and imaginative play plans. When children are allowed time and offered support to harness their own imaginations, their confidence to try out new possibilities is optimised. Within the safety zone of pretend play, all outcomes are possible, all perceived failure is tolerated and all ideas are explored. In this safe pretend world, nothing is final or decided upon so all is admissible as an option. And imagine if there are others with ideas and possibilities of their own to join your pretend play? A child that can lose themselves in this fantasy land of possibility, and can imagine a comfort toy or object as a companion, is in a state of mind that is most conducive to the early approaches of others seeking to be social with them. The potential to share and develop ideas comes naturally to children. When given the time to explore these ideas together, they become opportunities for young children to practise fundamental social skills as well, without difficult consequences.

Pretend play offers children a safe place to be wrong about just about everything and for it to be OK. It allows children to think creatively, react instinctively to their own and others' ideas, and to respond emotionally to new social dynamics as the ideas are developed. Pretend play is the place for children to practise how to remain stable in uncertainty – cognitively, emotionally and socially. It is vital to their future emotional resilience and their capacity for creativity that they remain open to possibility and tolerant of failing. As Ken Robinson said, '*If you're not prepared to be wrong, you'll never come up with anything original*'.[1]

The appeal of the crowd

This concept can be further developed when the importance of the peer group is reflected upon. A child's need to be with a companion, to maximise the opportunities of reciprocal interactions, may be why children believe that proximity to someone is a priority and why it remains a basic element of child friendship. When children first come together, they begin to make sense of their strange new environment with each other and friends are the source of meaning-making in this situation. As the source of meaning, they are also the source of relational identity, something which helps a child to render this wider world a socially manageable place.

All we, as practitioners and parents, can really do is model the emotional and socially acceptable boundaries we have learned for ourselves. These are all highly subjective and individual and are based on our own life experiences, both good and bad. They are influenced by our culture, our values and beliefs and these are reflected to children by the way we talk to and interact with others. Ultimately, we can only hope to have nourished children's self-esteem enough and that they have encountered enough practice to develop the emotional resilience and social skills, so that when an interaction or relationship they encounter makes them feel bad they have the capacity to transform how they deal with and react to it. They need to have practised the social skills that ensure they are emotionally secure enough to be temporarily disliked by another, and be secure and resilient enough to bear the fall-out of that happening. Often, once children begin to socialise in a wider world, their peers and their values can often have a great impact, particularly as they begin school. This is because peers are often sharing a perceivably more comparable experience and this makes them more useful as emotional points of reference for children.

Contingency friends

As children become more sophisticated in their friendship strategies, and more mature in their social and emotional development, they begin to practise for themselves the moral 'rights and wrongs' they have had played out in relationships around them. Often children can adopt contingency friendships. They do not necessarily align themselves with these friends but know that these are people who can be called on to be a friend in an emergency. Very few young children have had much time alone, and in these early stages of learning to be socially resilient, actually being alone is to be avoided at all costs. This phenomenon in itself can bring the unlikeliest of characters together as 'friends'. Young children will bounce in and out of friendships, and to many adults, these can appear flighty and unsatisfying, with big emotional and moral investments flippantly dealt with. But in these early self-chosen groups children are practising the social skills they come to rely on all their lives.

Watching Isaac

It would be remiss of me to write a chapter entitled 'Seeing children talk' in a book about their social development without exploring the importance of assessment and how important and useful it is in our work with young children. (I bet your eyes glazed over before you finished that sentence.) Of course the work we do with children is only strengthened by high quality and purposeful observation of our children, whether they are recorded or not. I could describe the benefits of, and the tools for, assessment and recording what we see and observe children doing, but this would be a superfluous addition to the many informative frameworks and constructive guidelines that already exist. Instead, I want to explore what we don't see, what we subconsciously ignore and, whether we like it or not, what we have been programmed to miss when watching the youngest of children.

I found a video made by the DfES in 2007 of what appeared to be an example of really good observation and assessment practice for a teaching session. It was of a teacher scribbling away on Post-it notes about the activities and conversations while watching a group of children playing with plastic animals in a sandpit. There was a plank across the sandpit and bricks at one end of it. Her notes contextualised the play as she scribbled, '*Jayden builds London Bridge using three bricks, counting them out and by using both hands*'. No doubt she would later be able to use this simple observation to substantiate fine motor skills, mathematics, knowledge and understanding of the world and probably something about how he was playing cooperatively with others in her formal assessment.

I was discussing this observation technique with a group of foundation degree students, using this video. When I asked them '*Who was watching Isaac?*' many of the students were not sure of who I meant, so we watched the clip again. Throughout the clip there was Isaac, loudly whooping and attention seeking by moving across the front of the teacher and darting around the sides of the sand pit. Three times he attempted to grasp the attention of the teacher, shouting '*Look at my elephant whoo-ing across!*', with an annoying '*whoo-whoo*' noise. Eventually, the teacher says to Isaac '*Ooooo Isaac, that noise!*', and we watch him leave the group to go and play alone. Who will understand why Isaac doesn't want to come tomorrow? His dismissal by this teacher may be the third time Isaac's exuberance and imagination had not fitted in with the group activity this week. As a student group, however, we had treated Isaac with the same disdain while we had observed the clip; three of the students had even commented on Isaac's behaviour the first time round.

The example demonstrated that even though we are, as practitioners, often tuned into how we can use what we see and hear what children around us say, if it doesn't fit with our plan or purpose, we can be guilty of ignoring or even dismissing them. The teacher in the clip could have redirected Isaac's cries to include animals in the play by the sandpit and the bridge. It would not have taken too much imagination to make the London Bridge take you to London Zoo, a missed opportunity for all involved.

Lessons

We would do well to retreat from such a prominent requirement to collect such volumes of 'necessary' evidence to substantiate progress and outcomes, not because we are uninterested or do not wish to inform ourselves about children so as to improve what we offer them. But we do run the risk of over-analysing some aspects of assessment and completely missing others. It also needs to be remembered that another person's perspective of an experience can only be guessed at. Our adult view of the child's intent in play or behaviour can only ever be subjective, tainted by our views, values, beliefs, experiences, agendas and purpose. There is no such thing as objective observation. We would do well to remember that: '*The significant moment is that when the child surprises himself or herself. It is not the moment of my clever interpretation that is significant.*'[2]

Rinaldi also highlights how children need opportunity to figure things out together separately from the adults, since 'their' childhood is a version shared only by those in it. The 'other' perspective of what they do, think or perceive is only ever just that: a perception, not a stance based on experience.

Having the trump card

So, if actions are said to speak louder than words, what action has the loudest noise? Giving children attention. Often I have heard parents lament how they are unsure of how to get through to their child. But they have the trump card and do not know it! It is their attention to their child that is the key.

As a practitioner, you can, at times, feel powerless to impact on the behaviour of a young, motivated, zestful and wilful child, particularly when you have the wishes of the parents, of course, directing all that you do with their child. I have heard practitioners in early years settings say how they like working with the babies, they are sweet, but that they prefer slightly older children because '*you can get so much more from them*'. This is often translated as 'they are more ready to learn' by teachers. It is this more finely tuned ability to be reciprocal with attention that is found in slightly older children that babies need to learn from us! They need to learn that to get a reaction from another person, an action from them is required.

Babies are no less reciprocal or capable of seeking attention than older children; it's just that we have to work harder to access their meaning, and that the gratifying payback of reciprocal interaction is less accessible. As practitioners, we have a duty to remain attentive to all children's and, in particular, to babies' attempts to communicate. With babies it can be difficult for the adult to stay interested because they may not receive an obvious response. But for babies, whose earliest attempts to interact with its environment can so hugely impact on their future sense of self-worth, it is critical that any early communications are positively acknowledged and responded to. The structure of what social interactions can be for every individual has its foundations in these earliest communication episodes.

Getting your attention

Language, and children acquiring it, is fundamental to maximising the speed and impact of the response they get. Let me give you an example.

A child climbing up onto a table is an inappropriate action in many contexts. Imagine the child who has developed a way to get a guaranteed reaction from his adults by doing it. It is not a positive reaction he gets, but he does not care since he cannot yet differentiate the good from the bad reaction, but knows that the attention he gets is definite and repeated each time he does it.

A different approach is needed to change the course of this repeated pattern of action for the child. Remember the trump card, and that it is your attention that is the social 'kick' the child is seeking, so withdraw your attention from the proceedings.

The vocal noises that the child makes will initially increase, in relation to the attention he is not receiving. Watch him: he will push boundaries to elicit the expected and wanted response from you. He will loudly complain, shout, wail; but he will also stop periodically to allow you to interject with the response he was expecting. Don't give it! The wailing may get louder, he may be older and be able to compound his objection to not getting the attention, with another action he knows gets a response from you. Screeching, provoking a sibling, grabbing and throwing in frustration; all these actions are intended to get a response.

The moment he stops, gives up on an action, retreats from the first or subsequent action and or the accompanying noises, or makes a far more appropriate action, we can give him the attention he craves. The unexpected attention at this juncture will result in noises and sounds of its own, usually far more tolerable.

But whether it is the delighted squeaks of the child who has managed to convey his needs to you successfully, or this child whose frustrated behaviour has been noisy and emotionally draining, the social common denominator is the desire to get your attention.

All the noises, eventually to include speech, are learnt to elicit attention – both positive and negative – from others, as quickly as possible.

Keeping the attention topped up

Good quality and a regular dose of focused and reciprocal attention for all babies and young children can keep their need for it topped up. The emotional energy that being social uses needs to be replaced and reinforced. Before young children are able to self-regulate their emotions and their own emotional needs, it is crucially important that this emotional succour is available for them at all times, from somewhere. It needs to be unconditional and genuine.

This is a crucial time for watching children and responding to what we see them say. Recently, with a very tired Lewis, I put him in his high chair for fish pie and peaches for his dinner. As a favourite, 'always eaten before' option, I was hoping for a quickly filled toddler, a warm bath and early to bed.

But his crossness at being strapped into the chair was loud, distressing and emotional for us both. Knowing he was hungry, I cajoled him through six or eight mouthfuls, and then offered him his favourite peaches. This got even more tears, eye rubbing, body straightening until I let him out, wiped his hands and dished up my own dinner.

Within minutes of my sitting down, Lewis was up to the table, with fork, wanting to dig into my fish pie! I had missed his cue to be allowed to sit at the table by himself, opposite his brother and be left to feed himself. He was now all smiles, and had come back to the savoury pie, despite having had some pudding already. He finished a full bowl of fish pie, followed up with a bowl of his beloved peaches willingly, happily and without distress. I had missed what he was saying to me.

Challenges and dilemmas

Attention deficit or social frustration?

The frustration that the pre-linguistic child experiences when they do not get the attention or response they want for their actions is compounded by their inability to affect the response they get without language. Lack of language, which is often blamed for heightening the 'terrible twos tantrum', could also be a lack of emotional articulacy or vocabulary to express emotions and can also exaggerate an older child's frustration at their perceived ineptness. The poorly named attention deficit syndromes can stigmatise parenting skills and label otherwise well-rounded children. In fact, we all, as adults, have a duty to model emotional literacy in our children. In a culture where most things are down to someone else (see Chapter 6: Engaging with families), and where very young children are rushed through a childhood, is it any wonder some struggle to keep up with the social skills required to 'succeed'?

Conflict-weary children

Conflict over dominance between young children is frequent and typical, but it can be really wearing on them, even when they encounter it in a pretend context. How do we help them to deal with it? The signs of it happening for them can be overreaction and upset within their play, and sadness, tiredness and lethargy afterwards if not resolved. Prolonged periods of unmanageable social upset for a child can make them angry and lonely. But as a culture, is it our instinct to reinforce boundaries of play and behaviour towards others for the child/children and send them back in, or can we recognise when a break or change to the dynamic is necessary? I would offer that in formal childcare and primary schools, the second option is less likely to be taken simply because of the numbers of children there can be to manage.

Despite my worry

At six years old and in Year 1 of the local primary school, Connor walks the short distance between the car and school gate by himself every day. Every day I give him the option to be accompanied and most days, and for some months now, he will ask to go by himself and offer to give me the thumbs up when he gets there, before he passes out of view and through the gate. With the school on the main road, several parents who have passed him have done a double take at him and commented to me how young he seems to be taking himself in to school. Some with surprise, some with disdain and occasionally one will say '*Gosh, he's good*'. But whether it is perceived as right or wrong, a safe thing to do or reckless parenting, nine times out of ten, Connor catches up with someone he knows, sometimes someone new to him, and is so quickly caught up in the chat that he completely forgets to put his thumb up to reassure me. What does more than reassure me, however, is that every day I see how he feels socially confident enough, at this young age, to find his own way into his world without me holding his hand.

CHAPTER 6

Engaging with families

'Nanny, were you born when it was a black and white world?'

Martha, four years old

We all have an opinion of what family is and about what our version of family values entails. It may include unconditional love, respect, 'holding in mind', loyalty, tolerance, grouping together in times of trauma or hardship and helping each other out when we can. It may mean feuding, long-held grudges, disappointment, loss of patience, control and upset. Behind all that, the cliché remains true: you can choose your friends, but not your family.

The young child's experience of their family will inform their own relationship values. Before they can verbalise their view, young children will be gathering information on how their nearest relate to each other and the behavioural strategies they see being used by the people around them. It is the wider world that Bronfenbrenner identifies in his social model, and this chapter will explore the importance of the interface between the child's home environment and the social world around them. The relationship parents and practitioners have with each other and the impact on the child's sense of security in new places, new experiences and with new people can be reinforced or undermined by the nuances of these adult relationships around them. For many children the childcare and early nursery settings often provide the first wider world contact outside their family unit of relatives and close family friends. The home environment and everyday reality of the child and their families can be reflected and complemented by the sensitive practitioner and teacher, not least by constructing positive relationships with the important people with whom the child lives. Have you ever heard a practitioner mutter something negative about a parent, or parent about a practitioner, in the earshot of the child for whom they both intend to have the best interests?

Looking in the window

For the practitioner, the child is the window into his or her family. We gather snippets of how life in this family may feel for this child from having family events played out in 'safe' role-play opportunities or the out-of-context questions asked of us by children. Recently, when I was asked where we all go when we die by a four year old I know, there came a long discussion about why people's bodies get burned. The child was concerned how hot that was and would it hurt the person being burned? Only when the child asked if I had ever been '*crimerated*', did I begin to understand what might be the poignant and possibly traumatic event going on at home. This was a more grownup concept; only the death of a family member or friend of the family could have prompted the use of such a word or concept at home. Children have just the same need as us to share their narratives, their stories. For this child, not knowing the term 'cremation' meant he was unequipped to seek solace, comfort or support for losing a much loved granny. This had left him unable to share his painful narrative coherently.

This view into a family must be respected and treated with discretion and professionalism. It is a privileged position and should be treated as such. Devereux and Miller describe the mother-minder relationship and the mutual respect that develops between them, making it a powerful agent for the child's wellbeing.[1] Based on a non-judgemental understanding of the choices made by mothers, the minder becomes 'in loco parentis' for the child. Despite the current culture to measure, assess, score and audit every aspect of care and education offered by a childcare provider, most mothers and parents would simply ask that you take a real interest in their child, care about them, and offer them something nurturing. Very few parents would ask that the, very often, highest qualified or most experienced practitioner sit in an office completing the monthly 'monitoring and evaluation' form. Instead, most would simply ask that their child's favourite adult be available to him or her during their time in the provision. How this administrative phenomenon came about is due to the high value placed on checking up on everyone, prioritised, it appears, above the importance of the needs of each child to have the best of care. The irony is that the media-defined 'nanny state' has left the children without the 'nanny'.

The essence of engaging

There is a lot of emphasis, quite rightly, on developing open, honest and successful relationships with the families of the children we care for. There are many reasons why this is paramount to both a child's emotional security and wellbeing.

The neutral assumption made by experiential educationalists, such as Ferre Laevers, is that a child's capacity and drive for learning is underpinned by emotional security and esteem. Currently called Wellbeing and Involvement Scales, this and assessment tools like it, are used to check the suitability of the soil for the seeds of knowledge and experience we intend to impart by teaching. I only use Dr Laevers's Wellbeing and Involvement Scales because they seem to link contemporary cultural values of childhood and currently fashionable educational philosophies together. Findings from the Layard and Dunn 'A Good Childhood' study of 2009 also demonstrated that there is a growing understanding of the integral part that wellbeing, esteem, happiness and health play in a child's motivation to engage with their life chances and education.

By nurturing positive relationships with parents and families, we may have deeper understanding of the nature of the soil in which the children grow when not with us. There is much respected work into the significance of the home learning environment provided at home on a child's wellbeing and his or her capacity for structured learning later at school: *'families who are otherwise disadvantaged can support good learning outcomes where they have provided a high quality home learning environment'*.[2]

This knowledge of a child's family and home environment should enrich and, perhaps more importantly, deepen the relationship and detail of concern that teachers and practitioners have for any one child.

Less person centred; more personable

The skill needed to connect with others socially is built around the skills of listening, a willingness to share yourself and demonstrate fallibility and weaknesses. It is not about power, priority of purpose or entitlement, but genuine, discreet and, above all, interest in another person. The practitioner who applies such empathic sensitivity to children takes time to know the child, and develop a deep understanding of them and their families. It is not self-seeking, but is based on being professional and tactful, whilst remaining non-judgemental and altruistic in purpose, on behalf of the child in its place within its family.

The practitioner who can identify with a child, their nuances and preferences, and can relay these openly, discreetly and with positive sentiment, often evokes trust and affection in a child's parent. They work and relate together on the premise that, to begin with, it is only the child that they have in common, and the practitioner invests effort into finding the key to the family dynamics. With this unspoken but hugely personal attention to detail, the most effective and highest quality practitioner instinctively recognises how to convey information about a child in a way that the family will positively respond to.

As a parent, you will be able to name the key person, childminder, carer or teacher who has emotionally invested in your child, and you will always have a strong memory of the benefit and richness they gave to your child's experience in childcare or school.

The practitioner or teacher who does not know their children and, what's worse, may not care that they do not know the individual child, has missed a crucial opportunity to develop the foundations for relationships with children and their families. These genuine relationships can be beneficial for the child and family and hugely professionally satisfying for the practitioner, thus providing its own raison d'être.

Causing offence

The current guidelines and checklists for outcomes, goals and strategies within which we, as practitioners, have to operate are manifold. They are there to provide a baseline for the effective, but not necessarily the highest quality, practice for those characters for whom such professional sensitivity is limited naturally. These frameworks are centred on child welfare and safeguarding, administration, monitoring, assessment of outcome and performance. And this is why so many of us are offended by the assumption that our practice needs to be policed in this way.

Policing relationships

Relationships with parents are no less policed. The framework for current early years practice[3] and the practice guidance for children's centres,[4] as the last formal guidance issued by the then government of the day, hold clear principles for working and engaging with parents. Reinforced by the Children's Plan of 2007, the guidelines promoted respectful and effective relationships, those which are built on a flow of information, a spirit of partnership and a foundation of diversity awareness. These are fundamental sentiments that any future frameworks for practice might cling onto. But the essence of the many practical ways in which teachers and practitioners intend to build relationships with parents can be condescending, cursory and, at times, barely polite.

Indeed, simply by stating that effective engagement with families is a target for all childcare settings and schools in guidelines and frameworks, for which evaluating statistics are no doubt faithfully recorded, the process of doing so lacks sincerity and genuine intent for the parent. Instead, it implies that the parents and families are to be advised of their inadequacies and how to improve, cajoled to join in or justify why not, or be a professional's 'casework'.

Hughes and MacNaugton described how, despite the well-documented benefits of parents, teacher and practitioners engaging with each other, the relationships between them are frequently '*too often strained and not very meaningful*'.[5]

The idea that the child, parent and their families are to be advised, cajoled to attend, persuaded or be influenced by the army of professionals that feel driven to engage with me as a parent in recent years, has disempowered the interested parent and distanced those less interested.

Hughes and MacNaughton indicated that problems arise largely from the constant '*othering*'[6] of parental knowledge by staff. This is when, regardless of a parent's relationship, knowledge or interest in their child or their wellbeing, the teacher or practitioner pays little, if any, regard for their expert status in their child's life. Such othering subordinates parental knowledge of the child to professional knowledge, making parents feel inadequate, subordinate and unimportant.

A culture of brokerage

A generation of parents has grown up in an era where there is someone available to do most things for you. We have estate agents to sell our houses, lawyers to sort our arguments and agreements, bankers and advisers to arrange our financial affairs, therapists to solve our emotional difficulties, and au pairs, nannies and childcare practitioners to raise our children. Entitlement and access to these, and many other brokers for the modern family life, are there for those who aspire to and can pay for.

In his thought-provoking chapter entitled 'Conscious Parenting', Bruce Lipton describes the seductive scientific argument of how the pre-programmed genetics of a child will unfold without much input, after parents meet a child's physical needs to feed, clothe and refrain from abusing them. It is a view that, he believes, is endorsing and perpetuating an increasingly lazy parenting phenomenon.[7]

Verny and Kelly further debate how frontier science is confirming that parents *do* matter, and that their impact on the mental and physical attributes of the children they raise is overwhelming.[8] The parent's influence on the blueprint of the child's behaviour is fundamental and lifelong. The discoveries of prenatal and perinatal psychiatrics and groundbreaking neuroscience are demolishing the myths surrounding what is understood about babies and their brains and, subsequently, the ambiguity of our impact on their earliest years.

However, the trend for brokering out aspects of our lives gives us, firstly, someone to blame when things go wrong and, conversely, a detached sense of responsibility about everything, including relationships. There is a socially tolerated period of time during which our youngest children display often defiant and sometimes difficult behaviours. Often called the terrible twos (see Chapter 2), the effort to consistently apply culturally appropriate social rules and model a 'better' way to behave towards young children can be exhausting. Whether it is right that this important role falls to someone outside the home or family is a dichotomy that will go on long past the interest in this book.

But it remains a common cultural practice for our youngest children to be placed in nurseries and with childminders as infants. This has been a consequence of the political drive for mothers to return to work, and incentives offered to place babies and young children in high quality childcare often for long hours at a time. This can mean that the important social referencing task of modelling effective relationship behaviour for our youngest children is frequently narrowed to the interface between tired parents and busy childcare practitioners.

And live on stage tonight…

As practitioners and parents, we are responsible for introducing children to the world, and equipping them with the skills to exist in it. If we acknowledge the importance of children feeling emotionally stable in the wider context, and also highlight the narrow point of contact with that wider world, then it becomes obvious how critical it is for practitioners and parents to model competent, effective relationships together.

For young children, the social implications of not acquiring culturally appropriate social skills are potentially for that child to become an emotionally over-reliant child who finds day-to-day negotiation and conflict challenging, and this will last long past the early years. This reliance on someone else to resolve their issues can result in a lifetime of learned helplessness for effective interrelationships. Of course, children need to have functional and positive relationships modelled for them to see, to know and feel how they work; but they also need room and opportunity to practise these skills for themselves. Only the adults around them can provide that. The parents', practitioners' and teachers' relationships can help to provide the frame for a child's future understanding of how relationships work. The shared relationships between children are also hugely significant. Often without adult-orientated agendas, child-to-child relationships are perfect places for children to share experiences together, practise social interactions and their early understanding of language. Most importantly, they learn to enjoy the company of others.

Figure 6.1 *The proximity of others*

The ease of productive relationships

Frameworks and guidelines that prescribe to practitioners, parents and professionals how people should relate to each other is at best distracting and, at worst, patronising and counter-productive. There already exists a strong undercurrent of distrust and superficiality between the UK education and healthcare systems and parents or patients. With parents described as users and customers, and schools and settings as service providers, the contemporary language used hints at the misplaced use of a business model rather than the business of educating and caring for young children.

Rather than parents being engaged with or directed, simple, more human, aspects of relationships are more useful in defining the features of well-grounded, genuine and functional relationships. It must be remembered that the child is not a commodity; instead it is very often a parent's most precious thing. At the very least, the fact that the parent presents their child to a practitioner for care demonstrates an acknowledgement that the child requires it. Establishing useful relationships with parents can only improve understanding of the significance of our joint responsibility to young children and their progressive development.

Empowerment

If there is a feeling that your effort and involvement can improve things, it provides both a sense of responsibility and ownership, but most importantly a sense of empowerment. Practitioners and teachers need to begin to see parents as allies in the raising of our next generation of children, and the relative experts of knowledge about their own child, and treat them as such.

Empathy

In Chapter 1, empathy was introduced as a crucial aspect of being a competent social being. Seeking another's view and moderating our own in light of another's opinion can be reliant on not just being sympathetic but empathic to other's needs, actions and wishes. Taking a moment to find common ground of understanding with a child's parent can generate good intention and break down barriers of distrust or apathy. I once saw a parent smack their child in a public place in front of other parents and children. What I did not do is make a public judgement of this parent's actions, compounding the negative situation with possible humiliation. Whether or not I agree with physical retribution for a child was not in question; what this family needed was privacy for a difficult conflict and understanding of the many factors at play in the situation. Judgement was not on the agenda.

Encouragement

Whether your personal viewpoint resonates with a parent's view or not, encouragement of their child in the skill or talents particular to them provides a personal touch of adding support on behalf of their child. One of the best-loved teachers

I ever knew had a gift for remembering tiny yet significant details of each child and invested real effort to connect with them and their parents regularly. Punitive accusations directed at parents, or unsubstantiated doubt in their children and their parenting skills, can only alienate them from those who make them feel inadequate, isolated or angry.

Endorsement

Similar to encouragement, endorsing the actions of parents and their wishes needs to be apparent. If this is not possible for practical reasons, these actions should still be respectfully considered in a timely way. We do not need to be overly officious in the application of policy to the point where it subsumes common sense. The application of such policies can often be cited by parents as patronising, unhelpful and unevenly applied. One of the two girls of a family in different primary classes of the same school had sickness and was sent home from school one Wednesday. Mum kept both girls home on Thursday, although neither of the girls vomited that day. Mum had been vigilant to limit possible contamination and kept both home, just in case, telephoning the school to record them both as sick for the day. On Friday morning, both girls were taken to the school gate where the Head allowed one of the girls through the gate but not the other. He did not seek details from the parent about the girls' health or whether either of the girls had been sick on the day of their absence. When challenged, his reason for not admitting one of the girls was that she had been sick 45 hours previously, i.e. less than 48 as is the current Health Protection Agency rule for sickness, and therefore could not come into school. He still did not check with the parent whether the other had been sick. To say this parent was angry with the inconsistent application of the policy was an understatement and her embarrassment at being stopped at the gate and denied entry did little for parent–teacher relationships.

Entitlement

Parents are entitled to have opinions about their children, their lives and the practitioner's place in it. Seeking information about their children is their entitlement, and should never be viewed as inconvenient or flippantly approached. There are always parents who will seek more of the practitioner's time than others, but the significance of their issue should be respected and managed appropriately. The Children's Plan was, at the time, an encouraging indication of recognition and significance of the parent in a child's early days. Its first principle was: '*It is not the government that raises children, parents do*'.[9] This principle was diluted a year later in the plan's 'one year on' progress report, perhaps indicating the complexities of the front-line difficulties professionals can have when engaging with all types of parents. It remains true that a crucial part of any practitioner's role is to be approachable, supportive and available to all parents.

Enjoyment

Children, their abilities and talents, as well as their characters and idiosyncrasies, should be celebrated and enjoyed. During the often action-packed, sometimes stressful and emotionally draining experience of life with young children, it is easily forgotten what a joy they can be. Sometimes parents need to be reminded how to take time to enjoy their children. Try telling a parent a funny anecdote, 'You will never guess what so and so said to me today?' about their own child and in front of their child. I bet they reach out and touch the child. Children can become the bridge between you and their parents, and your reminding them to enjoy their child will stabilise that bridge, offering positive social skill modelling to the child at the same time.

Enrichment

The emotional investment that high quality involvement requires when working with young children and their families is not to be underestimated nor can it be measured. I have read in past frameworks that practitioners are to project friend-liness but not become friendly. Sincerity is not a measurable professional attribute but an essential part of making others feel you genuinely care for them. You are either committed to a sincere relationship or you are not. Either way, children, if not their parents, will know and treat you accordingly. Be secure with immersing yourself in the relationships on offer with young children and their families. They are enriching, if not a bit daunting.

Endless

There are many transitions that children experience and it is a part of what you do for them to never put an end date on their relationship, or their parents for that matter. Transitional relationships are very important for social learning. The process of engagement and acceptance of others into their lives and later, from their lives, is a crucial life skill for children to acquire for themselves. Families will adjust to your introduction and your timely fading from their realities naturally, and in their own time. Your place in the children's world is borrowed for a short period of their life, whereas their parents will remain with them for all of their lives. Commit to them and their time in your life as a professional and, if appropriate, a personal influence on their lives. The timing for your significance in their child's life is not for you to define; all you need to do is your job, as well as you can.

Ambassadors and antidotes

Frequent interpretation of current political agendas in the media endorses the supremacy of the well-trained practitioner and teacher knowledge over that of the parent, perpetuating the idea of inadequate parenting being the norm. This can distance the 'good enough' parent further from feeling entitled, equipped and empowered to take part in their child's wider world.

Whilst working with a young family who wanted to place their disabled son into a 'normal nursery', as the manager of the setting, I found myself in the intermediary role between the multidisciplinary team making the decisions and the parents. This young boy of three years old, I will call him Sam, was never expected to reach his first birthday, and his physical needs meant that he had never taken a breath on his own without oxygen. His parents, and in particular his mother, had fought long and hard to secure the funding to support his many needs at home with his siblings and was now keen for him to experience other children in a wider world context. The multidisciplinary team had taken three months to come together, and the discussions around his care in our nursery came down to who would pay for the oxygen tank he needed to attend sessions with us. With people checking figures, budgets and funding streams, the decision was going to remain unfinalised. What stopped that being the case was this mum's sheer fight for her disabled son's right to acceptance, and as an ambassador for what she felt was most needed and justified for her child. She calmly and succinctly stated to this group of professionals, a group that might have been a daunting audience for her: '*Sam doesn't have time for you not to decide*'.

Maybe embarrassment or sentiment changed the course of events that day, but within two weeks I had undergone the appropriate localised training at his home, with his personal nurse and mum as the undisputed expert in all things 'Sam'. He started with a small group of peers in the main nursery three weeks after the meeting, but we waited another five months for the oxygen tank and carry bag he needed. Instead, we had yards of oxygen tubing line the nursery during Sam's sessions. Some days, mum would stay to enjoy her son in nursery, but very quickly Sam gathered a cherished practitioner for himself and a little group of peers who volunteered to be his tube and tank police. This practitioner went off to mainstream school with Sam as his one-to-one support, and became part of Sam's 'family'.

Mum recognised me outside a hospital a couple of years ago, while pushing Sam in his wheelchair. He was now eleven, and although he did not recognise me, she reminded him of my name. She shared with me how her personal relationship with Sam's father had faltered, but how Sam was enjoying a life full of friends and school, just as she had wanted. I felt genuinely delighted to hear it. There were clearly many sacrifices she had made, and was still prepared to make on behalf of her son, and her influence as her son's ambassador had shaped both his and my life.

Perhaps parents should be actively encouraged to ask for help from the professionals during times of potential crisis. By developing the kinds of political policies and personal relationships that make it 'safe' for them to do so, we can maximise the value of our relationships and work with all families. Practitioners can become the antidote for the emotional distress that the busy and seemingly uncaring world can sometimes have on young children and their families. We are ideally placed to challenge discrimination, stereotyping, negative perceptions and values about things that children may be developing, either reinforced or discouraged by parents. This will be further explored in Chapters 7 and 8.

Challenges and dilemmas

The parent as a 'service user'

There is a current trend to refer to parents as service users of facilities offered, particularly in children's centres. It could be argued that the parochial business model necessary to run the centres does not provide the kind of *human* approach most parents may want to encounter with their young children.

The need for referees

A culture of brokerage encourages in our children a reliance on a referee in their relationships. What used to be a 'tell tell tit' is now the older child who must inform an adult when a relationship or an interaction becomes tricky or out of their comfort zone. This same child risks never being truly able to negotiate or mediate their own affairs or interactions.

We need to nurture in children the traits of being resilient in times of adversity, developing a sense of 'stickability' and the skill of being grounded and level headed when dealing with life's difficulties and relationships. Practitioners and parents are the undisputed front line for this crucial task. Many shy from the responsibility, some deny it exists as '*they all go through this stage*' and '*they all get there in the end*', and others see it as the pivotal purpose of their professional lives with children. It exists, it is crucial and it is down to us. Chapters 7 and 9 will further explore these key social skills.

Whose job is it anyway?

Raising children is not only an individual family responsibility but also one for the wider society. If you were a parent needing help with your baby or young child, about any issue from health to behaviour, what would encourage you to ask for help? Answer that, and you will begin to untangle the subtleties of effectively engaging with parents, for the benefit of all children.

CHAPTER 7

Embracing differences

'How will you know who's who if we all look the same?'

Daisy, six and a half years old

There is no being less judgemental, racist or status conscious than a baby. But it is a very small window of blissful ignorance for them to enjoy. In a society, there are many expectations on the youngest of our children. Socially, there are many communal rules they have to grasp, from how to behave at meal times to sharing what is theirs with others. For many cultures, there are distinct periods of time offered to children where tolerance is given during their practice of developing mature social skills. Known as childhood, it is the time in which society considers that young children should develop the skills of social appropriateness within the culture in which they exist.

Is it really surprising that the time when many of these rules start to become important is during the toddler years? Maybe the natural cognitive pruning, that recent neuro-scientific research has discovered happens during the second year of a child's life, might not be the only factor at play in the challenge this period presents for the child and their adults. I too would find imposed restrictions on what I like to do frustrating, particularly when they don't make much sense to me. Why can't I walk around munching on my favourite snack? Or drag my spade from the garden across the light-coloured carpet of the house?

Learning social skills

During the first year or so of life the child's neural activity is busy with, first and foremost, solidifying the behaviours needed to guarantee food, warmth and physical safety. These primary elements, identified by Maslow in his hierarchy of needs, become the sole purpose of the physically vulnerable infant. It is also the period that is recognised as the window for developing secure attachments and establishing enough early skills to survive. There are government policies that reflect the significance of this time with maternity leave for parents and child tax benefits.

After this brief early period of innocence and gender neutrality, the emerging will of the infant signals a child's step into toddlerdom. Just moving from the name

Figure 7.1 *Why not chocolate hands?*

of baby to toddler is not something that children have any conscious understanding of; it is our adult classification. With this reclassification comes a change in our expectations of them. This time is, in a Westernised, masculine culture, often characterised by tantrums, contrariness and lots of episodes where the toddler seeks independence and expresses opinions. It is also the time that the adult world around them begins to enforce the rules of society and the expectations of their being part of the wider social community. The idea of society, political or otherwise, suggests control of someone, or rules determined by that someone over others.

It's a baby!

Often the first question we ask when hearing of a new arrival is whether it is a boy or a girl. We cannot help ourselves as it is one of our most instinctive classifications of another human being. But this is an adult phenomenon only. Babies and young children have no concept of their individual identity within the society into which they are born; they develop this.

But how early do children know whether they are boys or girls? What does that mean in a contemporary context? As children begin to identify with their place in the world, they begin to become aware of how they need to behave as girls or boys.

In her book, *Pink Brain, Blue Brain*, Lise Eliot warns us of being blindfolded to the scientifically based understanding surrounding sex differences and the neuro-science evidence that appears to support it. There is now wide acknowledgement that there are differences attributable to being either of the sexes. Biologically speaking, men and women are different, their brains are different, but as Eliot states, *'nearly all of the evidence for sex differences in the brain comes from studies of adult men and women'.*[1] In contrast, the neural plasticity of young children's malleable brains means that their sense of social and gender identity is anything but 'hardwired'. And yet, culturally, we have endorsed many differences as being innate and fixed by nature.

An adult phenomenon

Categorisation of others is important to those in the adult world but not children. Even very young children are aware that it is significant to adults, though it is a long time before they understand why. Young children themselves are sublimely naïve to the symbolic and representational classification clues on offer.

A young child at a local nursery had beautiful blonde hair to their shoulders and was often dressed in play clothes of many colours. The child's name was of South African origin and unknown as either male or female to the adults around them. Although the parents were certainly not attempting to raise the child as 'genderless', it was quickly apparent that it was the adults who struggled with not knowing, as fact, the gender of the child, including me. When I asked my child whether the child in question was a girl or a boy, he told me, '*She's a boy, mummy!*' It left me with having to ask myself why it mattered. Would knowing have changed how I would behave with or speak to the child? Probably it would.

Children, in contrast, are still developing the early cognitive skills required to begin to catalogue new information. They do not yet have enough knowledge of the world to need a complex filing system and the consequential group classi-fications and stereotypes we can be guilty of as adults. Their perspective is often described as seeing the world anew, it is fresh and uncluttered, and crucially, they are not yet applying values and opinions they have not experienced first-hand.

There are many examples of this freshness with which children view the world and their early awareness of classification of those in it. One of my favourites is the little girl who, when she first encountered a child of African descent, began to draw people with black faces and white limbs, or with black limbs and white faces. She never verbalised how she was reconciling this new information but her pictures demonstrated how she had had her perspective widened through her own real-life experience. Another example was a four-year-old child who, when a new family of Sri Lankan origin joined her school community, asked her mum '*Mummy, what colour am I?*' This again shows how, naturally, young children have no previous experience on which to base their response to the new differences they encounter.

Imagine being the same

Children are different to adults and women are different to men. Old people are different to youngsters and the teacher is different to the learner. Of course this is stating the obvious, and we know that the perspectives of those 'others' to us is different to our own; they must be – no two people's experience and lives can be the same.

One of the most important social development stages in becoming a socialised adult self is to learn to take the role of '*the generalised other*'[2], meaning to be able to imagine being many others in many situations. It means being able to imagine yourself as someone else, imagine their view or perspective or experience. This skill is at the root of empathy and understanding, and a cornerstone of sophisticated social prowess. It does not always follow age or development stages, but there are fundamental elements that need to be rehearsed, practised, played out and revisited by the child before it becomes adept at being able to consider this empathic view of another. For our youngest children, who have yet to gather lots of real-life experience, their imaginative drive to explore the possibilities of other perspectives is through unfettered play. For them, the real and fantasy are the same thing, all unexperienced, all possible. Through role play and fantasy play, children are imagining being someone else and what it may be like to be that 'other'. The safe space for trying out an 'other's' perspective deepens understanding and the ability to relate, and crucially, underpins a tolerance and acceptance of difference.

Reinforced by language

The positive and negative associations we all hold about gender and other social roles, values, ideals and stereotypes are all, without exception, underpinned by language. '*Language is not neutral. It reflects the cultural values and is a powerful influence on our perceptions*'.[3]

The attitudes, behaviours, beliefs and conditions children experience and are exposed to creates their understanding. For example, when considering gender, '*…while it is a biological fact that women give birth, it is a social construction they are the main childcarers*'.[4]

There are many examples of how language expresses assumptions made about being female or male. For example, why is it 'a gentleman's agreement'? Have you ever assumed the doctor is male and the midwife a female? In fact when two-year-old Albert was taken to the doctor, he said '*That not Doctor; that lady*'. Do we still use the term policeman and fireman over their female alternative? Have you ever been to a wedding and thought why isn't it 'I now pronounce you woman and husband'? It is a cultural habit that a man is referred to as a man, and a woman is often still referred to in relation to a man.

Pink and blue worlds

It was Jessie Bernard who defined the 'pink world' of young girls under the age of five, contesting that boys and girls are treated and talked about differently from birth and that the different expectations of each of the sexes determine their later sense of identity with their own gender.

Every child begins life with a gender and children quickly know that biological gender is fixed and not fluid; but the trying out of the language, attitudes and behaviours of the two genders is a much longer process. This period is described as *gender stability*[5] and the cultural roles, stereotypes and ideals begin to offer children *gender constancy*. This is when they establish that they are male or female and that this fact will not change. They become aware of a set of features or characteristics that they identify with being either male or female. Eliot describes how '*growing up as a boy or a girl is like being immersed in one of two different languages from birth*'.[6]

The importance of the language used about the gender groups, their characteristics, roles and identities in any given culture, is fundamental in defining the associations that children use to identify themselves. Young children are still establishing a view of themselves in relation to others.

Gender role reinforcement

Perhaps both men and women are only as different as a society made them, and that biology is destiny. However, the influences of powerful consumerism and media and the technological phenomenon of our contemporary culture offer many social clues and messages for children, both overtly and subtly, about how they should relate with their wider world. Everywhere we go there are very clear messages about what being a male or female constitutes in our culture.

Take clothing as an example. Clothing for girls is often pink and pastels; it portrays them as angels or princesses and even sometimes mimics styles more appropriate for an adult female form. How many five year old girls require bras? They are out there. As for the boys, their colours are blue, red, strong primary colours, with sentiments regarding noise, monsters and trouble. Do we mean it? Are we aware of it? How often have you heard girls be praised for being gentle and boys for being brave? Why do we pick these characteristics for the gender groups? Should we challenge them?

Another strong influence is that of television and film. For pre-literate children, the characteristics and temperaments of fictional characters can reinforce cultural stereotypes. Have you ever questioned why Princess Fiona is portrayed as being distressed for being an ugly ogre and Shrek is a solitary, intolerant, grumpy but lovable rogue? The female character is worryingly defined by her looks and the male has some depth to his character and offered supremacy in the story.

Society says

Developing gender constancy provides a fixed cognitive foundation for children to begin to learn how to become socially competent in the gender they are. They are driven to establish the social behaviours appropriate for their gender in their culture. In a Westernised culture, gender is fundamental to social order as a whole, and the intensity of focus on gender makes it one of the first senses of self that children develop. Social learning theorists believe that a child learns their gender because they are rewarded for behaving in gender-appropriate ways.

Return to clothing for a moment and consider swimwear. Why does little girls' swimming attire imitate that of the grown female form? Or shoes: why would small girls need high heels? These are indications of our societal endorsement of the early sexualisation of our children, particularly our young girls, through clothing, media and music. Even by offering relationship and sex education as part of the national curriculum, we are racing our children into being aware of their bodies in an adult way.

Being aware that their bodies are different to others and accepting this is one thing, but offering physical ideals through imagery, icons and celebrity that can rarely be achieved, is not helpful to young children to whom 'fitting in' is everything. The impact of this uncensored world of imagery remains unmeasured and unchecked. Is it a coincidence that the tragedy of eating disorders is affecting predominantly young pubescent girls as they struggle to reconcile their self-image with a sense of identity and self-esteem?

The public and private worlds

Earlier than for boys, girls are drawn into a public arena through this cultural phenomenon of early sexualisation. Perhaps long before they have the cognitive maturity to cope with it, their physical appearance gathers public interest, either through fashion, concern for their moral safety or protection from the potential negative consequences of having been born a female. But the influence of adult perceptions on young children about being born male or female begins much earlier. From a recent incident with my oldest son, who is in Year 1 of the local primary school and enjoying the development of a wide range of social relationships, I have had good reason to refocus on the significance of the different influences other children's worlds can have on our own children and those we work with.

A fellow school-run mum and I have developed a private joke about how our two children get on so well we should probably just buy our wedding hats now; it would be so much cheaper and less fraught to marry them off now. On a social networking site that we both use, she posted the following

Emily (her daughter) to mum: *Connor has dumped me.*
Mum to Emily: *Ahhhhh, what are you going to do?*

Emily to mum: *I will just go and find someone else* (with a shrug of the shoulders)
Young love = So simple x

Since Connor is unaware of the comment and the concept of PC spaces for adults to discuss things via social networking sites, I chose not to repeat this interchange to him in the way it was written. Instead I asked him who of his friends he had been playing with today? He tells me, but this list does not include Emily. So I ask him, what about Emily, have you played with her today? Connor immediately bursts into tears and I ask what is wrong. He tells me that she won't play with him and said, 'I think she is dumping me'. I give him a cuddle and ask him what dumping means. He tells me it is when someone decides they don't want to play with you.

Really caught off guard by his reaction, I did my best to comfort his hurt feelings and settle him for the night. I relayed the incident to dad. We were both surprised by the depth of Connor's reaction, and started to unpick the more subtle connotations of the incident. To respond to my friend on the site, I wrote

Just spoke to Connor about it and he burst into tears, for real. He says 'it is breaking my heart because I think she is dumping me!' It was really sad, and I have told him to hope they can still be friends. Bless x

Her response was to comfort and reconcile things for them both, as was mine, and she posted,

Oh bless him! I expect they will sort it out and the marriage will be back on by the end of tomorrow. Maybe young love is not so simple after all.

This was the end of the public posts but when I next saw my friend she asked if Connor was all right, and I asked the same of her about Emily. Her mum also relayed how Emily had later said that she chased Connor but that he runs away from her. Emily's mum had suggested to her daughter that she may be scaring Connor, and again, the incident became a private joke between us.

The incident became an uncomfortable memory for me for the rest of that week. I had a niggling feeling of how I wanted to be the gatekeeper of the negative feelings Connor's social development may bring him in contact with, and how this had been a stark reminder of the differences between children, their families and their differing, equally valid, values.

What it also highlighted was just how the interplay between the adult and child world endemically links one to the other. The more grownup concepts of our adult world are there for the knowing, if not yet the understanding, by children. A couple of school runs later, another concerned mum stopped me to ask how Connor was. I asked her in relation to what, and we discussed the appropriateness of the recent social networking exchange that had happened. Her concern about the incident was that the children were too young to be aware of these concepts and that we should be careful of polluting their understanding of social behaviour with concepts of more adult concern.

I reassured her of Connor's wellbeing, and we shared an ideal of protecting our children's innocence for as long as possible. What was poignant about the discussion was that this parent had naturally assumed that the language contained in both the public and adult posting and in my private conversation with my young son was the same.

All of us, as the parents of young children, were responding from a place of genuine concern for our own and other children's wellbeing. This incident had highlighted an imbalance in understanding about couple relationships in two friends, as well as an underestimation in the impact on their emotional response to that imbalance, for both children.

Our own, differing values had influenced our reactions to the incident. This is no less true for all young children and the social incidences that happen for them. Navigating this more sophisticated social referencing that needs to happen as children get older, and are exposed to more grownup concepts, is one of the trickier aspects of parenting and working with young children. The differences in social behaviour and consequences for that behaviour, as well as the differences in the language used to describe them all, can be a minefield.

Modelling and gatekeeping

We have a responsibility to be mindful of the impact we have on children, both as adults and, in particularly, as practitioners. Our language, behaviour, interactions and reactions to things are useful references to a child as they soak up the references provided, and develop an understanding of how things fit together. Our language in particular, as a means to communicate, is watched, heard and absorbed by all children. This duty of care is no more vital in our work with young children, in their current cultural context, than when we are representing the different genders, to them and about them. We are the gatekeepers to the responses a child has to their world.

Consumer children

Since complex mature socialisation behaviours are not yet fully understood by children, they assume that mutual status and respect for everyone is equal. They are unaware of the adult-world supremacy over children since they have no concept of the 'generalised other'. They believe what they are told by the advertisers and image makers. Before they are fully socialised they are unaware of the complexities and subtleties of the adult world and they do not yet know that they can not necessarily trust everything they are told, or sold, as being based in fact. This makes young children '*perfect consumers*'.[7]

With a consumer culture and media-rich contemporary environment for our children, it could be argued that they are exposed to often hugely stereotyped and potentially deficient perceptions of what their gender role or cultural identity is. The need for positive associations and, importantly, positive imagery and language used to represent all social differences is fundamental in our work with our youngest children. They have the key to future tolerance in society.

The modern-day childhood is not about children successfully adopting the historical gender roles associated with physical differences and traditional gender ideals from a time before feminism. Instead, our role is to dissipate the impact of the negative perceptions of modern-day media and the influence of unsubstantiated claims of supremacy by either gender, different cultural identity, or status of one over another. It is remaining mindful of moderating strong negative perceptions of any differences and encouraging children to determine their own place within the dynamics of the roles, values and cultural stereotyping they encounter. Maybe promoting and supporting societal sensitivities that endorse the importance of an individual's abilities and capability over their 'born as' gender and cultural or social identity could prove more enduring in producing well-grounded individuals for our future.

A new discussion to have might be how we, as educators and parents, can provide a gender-neutral backdrop of all things for our children, in education, advertising and entertainment. And if we were consciously aware of the profound impact our views, values and language has on the young children we work and live with, would we be more inclined to police it and its effects? This would, perhaps, begin to refocus our efforts towards endorsing values that increase the individual attributes conducive with any version of society that promotes tolerant communal living. What we need to model to our children are moderation and tolerance of all things and to celebrate all things different, and to nurture a sense of responsibility for the choices we make and values we hold as individuals.

The difference language makes

If language reflects and expresses the values and expectations of either gender in our culture, then understanding that language, and importantly why we use it, are fundamental. We continuously change the language we use to reflect our changing understandings of ourselves and our world. We can adopt any language to express how we find and understand things and, crucially, we can choose to change it and to create new terms as our experiences shape us. Wood suggests that

> Awareness of the power of language generates choices about what language we will use and support others in using. The choices we make affect not only our personal identities and lives but also social expectations and perceptions of gender. Thus, in being reflective about language, we assume an active role in shaping our culture.[8]

I will look at the powerful impact language has on us, our children and how it links our social selves with our emotions and our understanding in the next chapter.

The power of suggestion

Children know that being able to categorise others is important to adults, and will even try to find the 'correct' answer before they know it. During some recent reading time with children, we were enjoying the delights of Julia Donaldson's *The Gruffalo*.[9] It is a story of the meek overcoming the dominant with guile and humour. Whilst reading it, I purposefully used 'he' and then 'she' and then 'he' again for the mouse character. After we had finished, I asked the children who they would like to be. Lots of the boys said they would like to be the Gruffalo, with his scariness and 'raaahh' being the reason why. The children clearly labelled the Gruffalo as a male character, with 'jaws and teeth' a clear masculine physical feature for them to identify. Even though he could be thought of as the lead character, the mouse was not related to as a character the children would like to be. When asked if the mouse was a boy or a girl, the children were unfixed about it, with many changing their minds during our conversation. I had purposefully offered no language clues, and the children did not relate to its character traits at all. But as an adult, and if you know the story without looking, is the mouse a boy or a girl?

Once I had identified it as a girl, the children trusted my perception and adopted her as the clever little mouse who tricked the scary Gruffalo. My adult opinion and perceived position of authority influenced their thinking.

Actually, the mouse in *The Gruffalo* is genderless; there is no he or she throughout the book, so it is purely the reader's perception of characteristics that offers a gender. Powerful, isn't it?

CHAPTER 8

The links of language

'Why did the baker stop making doughnuts?
Because he got fed up with the hole business!'

Josie, aged four and a half years

Language links different aspects of development together. Josie repeats her joke to anyone that will listen, watching for their response, hoping to make them laugh. Cognitively, she is yet unaware that the joke is a play on words; she has yet to learn the phonemes or phonics to realise the difference between 'hole' and 'whole' and how that relates to doughnuts. She does not yet grasp the structure of the joke and why it is funny. What she is clear about, though, is the social pleasure that repeatedly telling her joke gives her, and her further delight in the emotional delight she experiences when she makes someone else laugh.

Without words, our emotional feelings have no name or expression, our cognitive understanding of concepts cannot be explained, justified or shared and our memories and narratives cannot be passed easily onto others. Doing such things are what makes us social, and language is at the heart of it.

If I asked you to think about your favourite childhood day out, you would remember the descriptions of the place, people and experiences of it. You would maybe label the emotions that thinking about it evokes, and be able to associate the smells and sounds of the occasion. Whether you say it out loud or not, all your thinking is in words, as the voice in your head links together the cognitive, emotional and social connections that your memory associates with my request. Language links our cognitive and emotional being to our social being.

I once worked with a practitioner who had never heard the spoken word, heard a song or a child laugh and, as someone who had been born deaf, she bought a new awareness to many of her colleagues and the children that she worked with. Her thinking was in symbols and shapes, as she would communicate in gesture, facial movements and formal sign language. Among the deaf community, not to stare at someone's face when talking is rude and to touch, tap or poke another person, relatively unknown to you, is socially acceptable. Her ability to communicate was not limited by her inability to verbalise; instead she was more consciously tuned into the body language and subtle signs we all use to convey meaning, which, in the hearing world, we stop relying on past babyhood. Her non-verbalisation was particularly engaging for the youngest of children, who were drawn to how she mirrored their heightened awareness of the non-verbal speaking we all do.

She, of course, would have been no less able to tell me of her favourite childhood day out; she still has memories, cognitive connections with sensory associations attached to them. It is just that she uses a different language to convey what she means to others.

Finding the words

The fundamental skill of using words to communicate is a life-long one that we begin to acquire from the moment we are born. It is a mainstay of being human and social. As a species, we use symbolic representation to convey meaning to others, and noise and speech are the shorthand to these interactions. Speech is a powerful tool as an aid to establishing emotional resilience and regulatory control of our emotions. It also means we have command of how we relate our emotions to, and respond to, others. It is no accident that young children are inherently motivated to develop language skills, since it gives them fast access to getting their practical, biological and emotional needs met. Being able to do this means they have an influence on what happens around them, and this becomes a cornerstone of their future self-esteem. Developing alongside these language skills are the cognitive and emotional frameworks needed for children to become the master of their emerging social skills.

Figure 8.1 *Bringing the skills together*

Language under strain

Once children have acquired the communication skills to competently convey meaning and language, rather than their noises and cries as babies, they can become the window to their emotional state. When a young child's language regresses to an earlier point in their development, such as babbling or adopting a babyish voice to accompany their words, this can often signal an emotional or cognitive period they cannot quite cope with. Outside pretend play, where it is entirely appropriate to hear many different tones and intonations and playfulness with language, a temporary step back to a more infant-like stage can often raise alarm bells. For many different reasons, the young child is seeking a more involved or concerned response. It may be due to a physical need that is affecting their ability to emotionally stabilise, or a social imbalance that is new or challenging to them.

Older children develop a deeper, more sophisticated understanding of their world and a more mature ability to relate successfully with it and those in it. When what is expected of them surpasses what they feel capable of coping with, one of the first signs is the loss of language. Children who express not just animated but exasperated language are either cognitively or emotionally taut. Like a rubber band, the tension that their situation is creating can be, if prolonged, exhausting for them and wearing for others. Struggling to verbalise their accompanying emotions is the essence of the angst children go through. This angst involves the social and emotional strain and imbalance we can all feel at times throughout our lives, but the effects are heightened for children as they are often experiencing them for the first time.

Our expectations

The conflicts caused by adult agendas and expectations on young children can begin alarmingly early, and at first glance might seem to be about adult control over children. Very young children are highly influenced by the adults around them, and will even seek out the perceived right answer or behaviour the adult wants. They have already learnt that adults expect it.

Unrealistic expectations of children can discourage them from exploring, experimenting and making the safe mistakes from which they can learn. Take, for example, the ten-year-old boy with a week's poor report card behind him. A boy whose behaviour has been cited at school as insolent and whose behaviour at home is erratic, wilful, disrupting and stressful for others. I expect his language has worsened too! He may be choosing to express himself angrily, or projecting negatively onto others; he may be shouting and screaming his emotional discomfort or may even have withdrawn from the exhaustion his emotions are causing. This older child is experiencing a new challenging social and/or emotional plateau and his rubber band is being stretched, and how he copes on the cusp of puberty and manhood will contribute to the blueprint for his emotional literacy for life. The strain for this child's brain is the same as any new social situation would evoke; the difference is our adult expectation of him.

This boy, like every child, needs to develop the social resilience and the interactional language to navigate new, ever more challenging social incidences. The early template his emotional experiences provide will be relied upon as the blueprint for future social behaviour, as he gathers evidence that either reinforces or refutes it as a successful way to interact with others.

Making the links

As adults, there is a whole profession of psychological specialists to help us to identify and positively manage our emotions. For young children, the learned patterns of how they regulate and cope with their emotions are yet to be determined. Navigating through more difficult social and emotional encounters, with support, provides crucial practice for developing emotional and social resilience and what become tried and tested coping strategies. These cannot be taught to children but it is fundamental that they are learnt. It is only through experience that they can gather the social skills to understand the consequences of their response to any given situation. Our instinct is to protect their feelings and interests, and solve any difficulties they have, but this has to be balanced with them gathering the skills to do this for themselves.

Language strategies

There are many language strategies that can be very effective in our work with children showing emergent language skills, but the most powerful is active and conscious modelling of how we behave to young children. A secure communication bridge between parents and practitioner can offer valuable opportunities to respectfully and, with an element of emotional safety, model how relationships and language can work. All adult examples of how to communicate are absorbed by the children who see them. Children learn from what they see all around them, whatever it is we show them.

Recently, a friend's daughter was experiencing her first taste of the playground threesome. Tricky for many young children, this is when a group of three repeatedly fall in and out of favour with each other to the point of upset as one of the three is rejected, only to be invited back in soon after. Unlike the contingency friends we see children have, this is more real and very personal for the children, as they try to make sense of exclusivity in their friendships. The social practice this experience offers children is invaluable but that does not make it pain-free, for child, teacher or parent. For the child, it provides emotional practice at feelings of disappointment, rejection, as well as experiencing trust and acceptance in relationships with others; but the process can be wearing and confusing at the same time.

For this girl, the playground upset was now intruding on her home environment, and her mother felt she was beginning to feel overwhelmed and exhausted. What she needed was a safe place to talk through her handling of the day's events, a place where there was no guilt, punishment, judgement or consequence. By engineering an opportunity for a replay of an emotional interaction between us, the mother and I demonstrated how we would approach discussing a sensitive issue around our feelings together. Although entirely embellished, and mildly uncomfortable, my feigned verbal admission of feeling vulnerable and hurt, as well as her mother's demonstration of sensitivity for my feelings as a friend, had the desired effect. This young girl had seen how it could be handled, and the openness that this safe place offered provided mum and daughter with a strategy to soothe the inevitable upset of this period of social learning for this girl.

Social and emotional habits

This early modelling of language structures begins much earlier than many believe. Stadlen and Gerhardt described the emotional value of offering babies comfort. They highlighted how the physical, emotional and unconditional comfort offered initially through the mother–child attachment provides a child with a template of how to return to an emotional 'normal' as a pattern for life.[1] By comforting an infant from upset to a more stable psychological state, the context of the trusting relationship provides a practice place for learning this important life skill. Eventually, young children will hopefully develop the habit of being able to soothe their own difficult emotions for themselves. Being competent at regulating our own emotions can influence a person's lifelong wellbeing, and their social resilience. The comfort of returning to a psychological and emotional balanced state provides a life-long blueprint for regulating intense states of emotional instability, as well as coping and managing more difficult negative emotions, such as guilt, bereavement and sadness.

Trust is also a benefit of establishing grounded social and emotional habits early on. To be able to trust others gives young children belief in their own social abilities, relationships and an early sense of their worth to others. The context of their earliest social relationships contributes to the child's proficiency for emotional self-regulation and their self-esteem later in life. This early blueprint of behaviour becomes the template for lifelong habits of mastery, and for subsequent social and emotional resilience, which follows from the self-belief that mastery induces.

Asking questions

Asking another person questions is an aspect of being sociable that can be informing and enlightening and demonstrate a genuine interest and willingness to become engaged with them. It requires practising empathy and sympathy, takes us out of our self-orientation to focus on another, and can, most importantly, help us to keep a perspective on our own emotions and feelings.

For the youngest of children, whatever their apparent language abilities, asking them questions can be a great diffuser of their own powerful early negative emotions; a child's demanding tantrum can be diluted if it can be distracted by a question. Rather than powerful emotional energy being used to shout and scream their dispute, a well-timed question makes them cognitively change gear. The peak of energy can be transmitted to seeking an answer, or at the very least, distracted from the upset as they become interested in the new encounter. You are speaking directly to their brains.

The technique of asking questions can be particularly useful to the experienced practitioner who may not be the most familiar adult for a distressed or upset child. Asking questions of a child triggers the activation of the blueprint because it requires the brain to go searching for a response as it revisits its back catalogue for information. It sends the energy of their brain to a reflective, 'the answer is here somewhere' mode. The familiar neural paths that searching for an answer finds, provides not only a distraction from what the brain was originally focused on, be it upset, distress or wanton destruction, but also can reassure the child that they have some control, mastery, over how to respond.

The importance of making mistakes

The capacity to make errors, to try one thing and reconcile the outcome when it does not have the perceived effect, is a central part of all learning. It is also central to being creative and inventive, and demonstrates a willingness to have a go and take a risk. Children are innately able to do this; it is the environment around them that ultimately harnesses this creativity as a route to new possibilities in under-standing, or discourages it in a culture where mistakes are not to be made. This trait is never more visible than children using early language.

During a family day out to a castle, a group of about twenty children were thoroughly enjoying being shown some medieval talents. Local volunteer enthusiasts had acted out a whole themed experience of Blind Man's Bluff, jousting, hunting and, most importantly, sword fighting, for children as part of the day.

It was during the sword fighting that the actor dressed as the mentoring noble told the children to shout insults at the peasant before they ran him through with their newly acquired sword skills. To hear twenty children loudly shout 'Insults' caused much amusement for the watching parents and adults, and it was delightful to be reminded that even without stability in understanding about the context or use of the language they were using, children are built to have a go, to be creative and to trust in others.

What is really important is acknowledging how we, as the adults in children's environments, react to the language mistakes they make. This is implicitly affected by our own values, beliefs and experiences and it would do well to be reflective of this fact, both as individuals and collectively. Children will have a go as their drive to communicate their meaning and interact with the world is more potent than their awareness of the social implications of getting it wrong.

Social interaction stability

The emotional stability and subsequent social resilience that young children learn have their roots in the earliest of the child's relationship experiences. Direct eye contact is a cornerstone of this, as are touch and verbal communication. All these are part of the process of developing trust with another person. *'They (babies) actually spend remarkably long periods of time just gazing into the eyes of their carers.'*[2]

Bowlby's theory of attachment between the infant and their main care-giver is a pivotal concept to many of the contemporary customs and ideals we have in current childcare practice. For example, breast feeding is recommended not only from a dietary perspective. The baby and mother are perfectly positioned during feeding to share eye contact and continue to deepen an attachment during this time. Other current practices includes favouring plenty of 'tummy time' for babies to encourage them to develop the strength and physical autonomy to seek interactions by moving their heads and bodies towards noises around them. By ensuring babies and toddlers have backward-facing buggies, we can offer them the opportunity to have the reassuring sight of their special person. Learning to do baby massage has become a fashionable activity, not only because of the nurturing power of touch between baby and carer, but also because it helps to develop a foundation of physical trust, including developing a complicit acceptance of direct eye contact with another. All these can help establish a foundation for future emotional and interactional security between baby and carer. Even once children have moved to childcare outside the home, access to an identified and trusted key person when away from their parent or main carer has become an ideal of most practice.

All these reflect the significance of interactions between adult and child as being reciprocal, respectful and with a measure of equal effort.

Getting down to their level

The effectiveness of asking the brain questions is totally reliant on the stability of the engagement you have with that person in the first place. As childcare practitioners, we are no doubt all aware of the recommended customary interactional practice of 'getting down to their level'. I have known otherwise promising candidates for recruitment in childcare falter when asked to spend time with the children with whom they will work. Their instinctive ability to connect with young children can be gauged when you see how they interact with them, or not. Being sensitive to the significance of respectful body language and also intuitive enough to read that of others are fundamental skills of the effective practitioner.

Intention and choice

The success of the social interactions we have with others relies on having a wide range of responses and vocabulary to articulate our intended meaning. The current National Curriculum places literacy at the heart of children's learning and development. This is in recognition of the fundamental significance of children developing a competent grasp of the language, grammar and vocabulary of the environment we live in, and its effect on the future life opportunities they will encounter. Language skills can determine a child's sense of efficacy, self-esteem and their sense of control, since they influence how we are able to interact with the world.

> *'Vocabulary at age 5 is the best predictor of later social mobility for children from deprived backgrounds.'*[3]

Children not only need to develop language skills but they need to be able to perceive the consequences on others of the language they choose. The time and opportunity for practising these skills is during childhood, with the opportunities for language acquisition closing around puberty. After that, our emotional and language deficiencies are likely to be negatively referred to, often blamed for a perceived lack of success or for some relationships faltering.

Digital days

Many of us already have reservations at the way the technological boom may turn out to have a negative influence on the language skills of the young children around us. Whilst acknowledging that the digital world is, and will continue, to be a resounding feature of their world, we must also understand where our own reservations come from.

Not only do we have distant, nostalgic memories of our own childhoods, of a time before iPads, iPods, avatars and text speak, maybe even before computers and mobile phones, we may also be unconsciously suspicious of any new technology that inhibits the frequency of face-to-face interactions. There is a growing concern about how we are all losing the skill for face-to face-interactions, conversation and negotiations, and perceive a negative impact on social interaction and relationships skills in our future generations of children.

It is well documented that there are concerns about the overuse of technology, at the wrong age, on a child's emergent language. Language is a gateway to new concepts, new understandings and, most importantly, a way to interact with people. There is no replacement for children being talked with and to by others who have a genuine interest and concern for the child's interests. Regardless of our technological environment, there is no substitute for getting two minds in contact.

> Language is something to do with the complex business of getting two minds in contact, because the exchange of meanings and language is at the heart of human communication.[4]

Challenges and dilemmas

Time, space and opportunity

The importance of offering time and space to the ideas of children demonstrates how we value them as individuals. It also provides opportunity for them to recall and rehearse experiences they have had, and play out feelings they may have about them. Time without space, or the other way round, can be frustrating for children who wish to explore ideas. To really young children, this is exploration with you close at hand. The language that happens with you as part of a child's first-hand experiences magnifies and enriches the social, emotional and cognitive benefit of the experiences. But this is not new information. Research from the Bristol Study in the late 1980s found that children learn language best, not through drills and instruction, but when adults attend to, and are genuinely interested in, what children are saying and when adults and children are committed to entering into real, contextualised conversation. There is little space for the time and opportunity needed for contextualised conversation within the overstuffed curriculum of the current education system. This is driving a renewed interest in teachers, practitioners, educators and parents for a less constrained, less prescriptive forum for young children's learning.

Face-to-face skills

There are contemporary concerns about the demise of face-to-face interaction due to the advent of digital and social media currently in use. Is it that the potential isolation from real interactions with real people undermines the value of the virtual experience? These concerns form part of the growing support for revising the current primary curriculum to include outdoor, physical, non-digital based, real-life experiences for children.

Even-effort interactions

Often, as adults, we learn how to seek out even-effort interactions. By this I mean those people with whom the relationships we share have become comfortable and stable with the passing of time and the sharing of experiences. We feel familiar, cared for and emotionally and socially unchallenged with this other person. Many of us, as adults, are not comfortable to meet new people and seek help to understand how we can improve our communication skills with others, either professionally or personally. As the adults in the lives of the children around us, do we not owe it to them to become the ones that they rely on, to give them familiar relationships that provide them with even-effort interactions, that are mutually respectful and full of social and language practice opportunity?

Meeting new people

Meeting new people is part of life; modelling this as a positive experience to children is important. For children, they inherently have curiosity in all new things and people; it is us, as the 'others' in their worlds, that often instil risk and fear into their social behaviours. One of the first junctions of meeting lots of new people can be a child's transition to school. It is culturally perceived to be a very big deal, and it is culturally accepted to make it a big deal for our children too. Yes, it is a new beginning, and yes, they will meet new people, and yes, it signals the end of the baby era of their lives for them and, crucially, for us. Children, however, do not hang on to shared experiences and shared meanings as their painfully nostalgic parents do. They have not yet had enough experience to need to hold onto people and places as a comfort; that is what we do as adults. It is us that need the familiar parents of familiar children to arrive on the first day of term at a new school so that we can meet new teachers, encounter new places and experiences together. How we behave and the language we use to talk about transitions, inevitable life changes, new 'normals' and how it 'used to be', models to children how they respond. Think about it. The fear of 'new' is learned.

CHAPTER 9

Ready for school, prepared for life?

> I believe this passionately: that we don't grow into creativity, we grow out of it. Or rather, we get educated out of it.[1]

As part of some research I conducted a few years ago, I explored the impacts and effects of young children entering school as early as they do. In the UK the admissions policies for many education authorities clearly specify that a child must be in full-time education from the term after their fifth birthday. In reality, it is common practice for the majority of young children to enter primary school during the September term after their fourth birthday. The small print of many of the admission policies remains ambiguous in dealing with the concerns of individual families that believe their children may be cognitively or socially unprepared to enter school. There is, in contrast, a very definite recognition by parents and practitioners of the children who '*are just not ready*' to join school.

This sentiment is often centred on concerns that are transparent and inevitable to anyone who has an understanding of the momentous growth and development that children undergo in the short twelve months between being four and five years old. For it is during this year, at different points for different children, that the pieces of the cognitive and emotional puzzles begin to slot together. They begin to consistently apply cognitive understanding to new problems and scenarios. They have independently initiated periods of prolonged focus on self-perpetuated tasks, and there are increasingly sophisticated communication techniques used within trusted relationships, as they practise their social interaction skills.

Harnessing potential

Skills are not age related; it is not my age that denies me the skills to be a top kite surfer. I would still have been too scared to try it even when I was six years old. However, for our youngest children there is a critical period of potency while they develop the life-long resilience and dispositions to enjoy learning new skills throughout life. The earliest years of a child's life sets the blueprint for a lifetime of successes and failures, both emotionally and socially. Harnessing children's individual potential is a time-sensitive process, and that process has to acknowledge the child's place and autonomy in it. The current entry to school arrangements suits some, but not all children, sometimes to the detriment of their potential and development. This, for some children, can be temporary and short lived when sensitively managed by practitioners and parents. For others, it can interrupt a child's emotional development and disrupt their trust in the world they know, affecting the people around them and undermining early seeds of emotional and social resilience.

Social resilience

Resilience is the ability to tolerate a degree of strangeness or instability. It is a child's mechanism for coping and their acceptance of the necessary transformation from one psychological state to another. It is this that determines how happy they will be along the way. Arguably a modern-day childhood is often about experiencing more and more instability in their social relationships. Be it due to high levels of parental separations and divorce or the increase in reports of a bullying culture, the social resilience of the youngest of children is being tested in many ways.

Social resilience is the capacity to continue to engage intelligently in relationships during times of emotional uncertainty. When children enter formal school before they can cope with it both socially and emotionally, it can cause distress to both children and parents. It can also cause concern in otherwise more emotionally resilient children, as they seek to understand their own, and others', reactions to experiences within the new context of the bigger groups in school. These aspects of emotional uncertainty for children and families can cause disruption and frustration for teachers and staff, as they attempt to find a common denominator of development amongst all the children in the group, in order to begin any structured learning provision.

Social junctions

There are many social skills that children gather throughout their childhoods, but one of the first and most significant milestones and the test of these skills is that of the transition from home to school. A child's grasp of the early concepts of cooperation and collaboration with others outside the protected family, and in a larger peer group, is crucial. This, combined with their early attempts to negotiate their way and communicate their individual thoughts, feelings and ideas, is no mean feat and, when successful, should be celebrated. The significance of the social relationships surrounding children is core to the way they cope with and absorb new experiences. The language used by others around them about school and the newness of it influences their perceptions, expectations and ideas; and it is these that begin a child's relationship with the environment in which much of their formal education will take place.

The purpose of school

Thomas Arnold, the headmaster of Rugby School in the Victorian era, believed that the purpose of school was primarily for the formation of character as a preparation for successful adult life. He believed that educational instruction promoted discipline and moral development in children. The post World War II years also saw a renewed focus on Arnold's *character education* as the citizenship of the nation's inhabitants was identified as a political strength. The most recently revised National Curriculum for schools proposes that the primary purposes of schooling are first that:

> the school curriculum should aim to provide opportunities for all pupils to learn and achieve[2]

and second:

> to promote pupils' spiritual, moral, social and cultural development and prepare all pupils for the opportunities, responsibilities and experiences of life.[3]

These aims demonstrate a contemporary political focus on the moral guidance of our youngest citizens through schooling. Most recently, there has been public debate about the need for a refocus on the development of character in children rather than exam results.[4]

To restate that building character in children during their school years is key to their life-long success suggests that somebody is struggling to keep this as a priority. As controversial as this may sound, the prize of public prestige for individual schools through Ofsted and SATS results far outweighs the quieter, more modest rewards of individual children finishing their education with their talents, imagination and enthusiasm for learning intact. The showy, public success of academic results, that seems to be so important to society, continues to perpetuate a 'one size fits all' education system. This is undermining our children's right to a socially and emotionally empowering learning experience that nurtures their individual talents in the institutions where they spend fourteen of their first eighteen years of life.

What is certain is that much of the more sophisticated social development that children experience will be within the context of the relationships they encounter at school. Erikson attached psychosocial stages to age, and identified several hierarchical emotional and moral development states that each child naturally goes through. For example, he loosely defined an age of six to seven years old as the period when most children were emotionally, socially and cognitively mature enough to grasp the concepts and implications of guilt and shame. Many of Erikson's states illustrate stages of a child's moral maturity.[5]

Moral education

What is considered to be right or wrong in any given society, or the course of action or choice taken by an individual, is a subjective judgement based on the specific context of that individual's experience to date. What each of us considers the right moral choice is contextualised by the societal conventions we are surrounded by, and the personal experiences we have had that reinforce their existence and worth to us.

Here is a family example. When Connor returned home from reception class with two small plastic collectibles, which were the current craze in his peer group at the time, I was dismayed by his blatant borrowing from another child. His justification in his negotiating the two most prized figures from this other child was sophisticated, and he was genuinely unclear of why I was clearly not pleased by his negotiated acquisitions. It was only after a protracted period of questioning did it finally emerge that his 'swops' for these two prized possessions had been two other figures from the same collection that he had stolen, from the same child! Within the adult understanding I have of society's conventions, stealing is morally abhorrent, but for my four and a half year old child who was witnessing lots of peers exchanging and 'trading' these prestigious pieces, the origin of the plastic figures was superfluous. He was even surprised that I was not impressed by his canny manipulation of another to secure them.

What this demonstrates is the same phenomenon that surprised Hartshorne and May in their research during the 1920s. They discovered that very few of the students they observed were virtuous, and that, instead, most children cheated, behaved selfishly, and lacked self-control a large amount of the time. Virtue, according to their data, seemed to be context dependent as students cheated or lied in some situations and not in others. They concluded that these were not character traits as such but instead: '*specific habits learned in relationship to specific situations which have made one or another response successful*'.[6]

In other words, regardless of the historical point of focus, the responses children get or believe they will receive for their actions are a significant and contributing factor in their future sense of moral responsibility and identity within the society in which they find themselves. It is our actions, or reactions, that make their actions acceptable, or unacceptable.

Making sense

Research on the development of children's moral understandings by Nucci has shown that morality begins in early childhood with a focus on harm both to the self and others.[7] Young children are concerned with their own safety as a basic biological priority, and quickly know that it is objectively wrong to hurt others. They come to understand that, even in the absence of a rule against hitting, it is wrong to hit and hurt someone because, '*When you get hit, it hurts, and you start to cry*.' They have personal real-life experience of the effect of being hit by another.

To them such a moral rule makes sense, but their grasp of fairness as reciprocity (treating others as one would wish to be treated), which is often what is considered moral in a wider socially conventional context, comes much later. Fairness for the young child is often expressed in terms of personal needs being met. '*It's not fair*', often means, '*I didn't get what I want*', or that someone's actions caused the child to experience harm. While young children have an intuitive sense of morality, they do not have a fully developed understanding of fairness. Nor do they have an understanding of the function of conventions in organising social systems. For educators to be effective in fostering children's moral and social growth they need to match educational practices to the developmental level of the child. This means that any rule needs to make sense to the child, before the child will even attempt to adopt it as anything to do with them. In order for the rule to make sense, the consequences need to be within the child's understanding. To be proficient at doing this with children, teachers and practitioners need training, a deep under-standing of child development and an experiential instinct for applying it. Above all else, they need to be trusted by the child. Establishing these deep relationships with children can be as rewarding as they are demanding.

The tools for sense making

Echoing the Labour government's priority in 1996 of '*education, education, education*', the tools for helping all of us to make sense of the rules that apply to our worlds are *language, language and language*. A competent grasp of words and signs is essential for successfully conveying meaning and explaining our inten-tions to others. As language and the acquisition of grammatical knowledge and vocabulary develop for children, there is an explosion of talking, as the practice of these newly acquired skills and knowledge begins. The urgency to use their new skills often dominates its accuracy. You do not have to eavesdrop for long before you hear young children adapt one word they do know to demonstrate something they mean but do not know the word for. From two-year-old Amelia telling me how her '*tongue has freckles on it*' when she was examining her features in a mirror, to three-year-old Lucy expressing her delight at the arrival of the winter's snow, exclaiming '*the snow is all glittered*', children will borrow vocabulary before they limit their innate drive to communicate their thoughts. As Gonzales-Mena says, '*language is the formation and communication of information, thoughts and feelings through the use of words*'.[8]

The disposition to express their intended meaning illustrates not only a child's in-built drive to socially interact with others, but just as importantly, their flair and imagination for new concepts and possibilities. This propensity for imaginative construction of ideas and a confident ability to convey these ideas to others is crucial as children move into school.

> Recent research has shown that language development at age two is very strongly
> associated with later school readiness, with the early communication environment

in the home providing the strongest influence on language at age two – stronger than social background.[9]

The rules of school

The natural and necessary constraints of many contemporary primary schools on the freedom and solitary interests of individual children are linked directly to the rise in the numbers of children in class groups. The school rules are often for the benefit of the group and the comfort of others using the same resources, facilities and communal spaces. For young children, it is not the constant close proximity of lots of other children that can hinder their expression of ideas; it is the limit of opportunity for them to stand out from their school crowd.

The early years at primary school are often the time when a child's need to imaginatively express themselves is naturally curtailed by a number of influences. First, many children have absorbed the social behaviour appropriate for the repeated routines of each school day. Many have settled into the school run, are comfortable and confident with the routine and rhythm of the school day and can consistently and independently function as individuals within the school context. They have developed early friendships and some strategies for dealing with the new social interaction experiences that these bring, including applying their early moral judgements to how they should and want to behave towards others. All this is set against their developing sense of individual identity whilst grappling with the group rules imposed by settings and schools. These all knit together to make an individual's version of common sense: the making sense of the common occurrence.

Put simply, young children are developing the social and emotional skills to cope with transforming from the very important person they are in their own early family experience, to being one of a large number of others being managed in a school environment.

Regardless of the quality of the school, its results, its place in the league table or its policies, the crucial ingredient needed for any child to make this developmental transformation is the social relationships they establish with the others around them.

The imaginative world of school

To harness a child's imagination and early sense of self-esteem, and yet apply the school rules effectively for the benefit of the larger group, is a dichotomy that often presents itself to many teachers and practitioners. If you have ever had to ask a child, who has spent the session engrossed in bringing an idea and creation to fruition, to pack away because it is time for the group to begin something else, you will have had experience of this. For many, this is too frequent a dilemma. The value of such free play, self-expression and imaginative exploration is widely understood to be significant for young children as they learn to persevere and concentrate, to try things out, perhaps fail at one perceived outcome, only to adapt the outcome to another, more stable idea. The opportunities for language development and social interactions are limitless. School, and the adults in it, have the unenviable job of balancing a child's zest and creative exploration with the needs of the bigger group, which can often mean the sensitive juggling of both priorities and people, within the restraints of policies and statutory requirements.

What is success and who measures it?

Success is a subjective concept but a contemporary perspective of it for children in England would be to reach their full academic potential in order to maximise their social mobility and life opportunities by having a 'good' education.

Lilian Katz proposed that for children to realise educational success, particularly in early years, a strong sense of self and worth is imperative. The biggest challenge for young children, and the adults that facilitate their learning, is to continue to harness a child's imagination and language development within a group context, whilst nurturing their individual self-esteem and talents, and by encouraging the dispositions that develop a child's engagement with learning for life. They need the social skills and emotional resilience to continue to hold onto the capacity for creativity and imagination they were born with, past their years of formal education and into adulthood. This can be simply translated into the child's propensity to 'have a go', and subsequent resilience to the social and academic implications of taking that risk and getting it wrong.

By providing a wider context to deepen our own understanding, I hope to offer a clearer perspective of our national position in a global context. Globally, 115 million children do not attend a school, more than 56 per cent of these are girls, and over two thirds of the world's 860 million illiterates are women.[10] Do we really believe that these children's lives could never be successful in any recognisable way?

The shared experience of friendship

In a landmark report for The Children's Society called 'A Good Childhood',[11] Layard and Dunn placed children, as their top priority for a happy life, someone to share things with. This was above every other possible want. A large proportion of children believe that the adults in their educational experiences are not there to play with them, only to be in charge, to supervise and to discipline them. In contrast, the other children that they play, interact and learn with, are sharing their histories and will share the cultural era in which they exist, as an influence on their lives, values and experiences. So if children perceive adult supremacy over them, the importance and influence of peers and childhood friends become even more potent.

A child's schooling experience and the relationships they have with friends provides the space for learning many important social skills. Through their sharing of experiences young children can begin to develop a shared identity without losing the early version of their individual selves. This becomes particularly relevant as children become independent of their families as their sense of identity within a community is strengthened. This can lead to a strong sense of personal responsibility for their actions in relation to the impact their actions have on others.

Another valuable aspect of friendships for young children is that they often provide the opportunity to safely experience and practise the more negative aspects of healthy social relationships. The value of practising conflict under the watchful eyes of attentive and sensitive adults at school helps children to develop more mature social skills that will remain with them for life. To have secure relationships within which disappointments and difficulties are both tolerated and coped with, lend children valuable experience in coping with relationships on their own in later life. The social phenomenon of school offers children the opportunities, both good and bad, to practise social and relationship behaviours within the cultural context of the environment they live in. Children of each school generation are learning the skills of existing communally with those who inhabit their worlds.

Technology v. language

The overuse of technology is perceived to have had an adverse effect on children's emergent language and to be linked to the demise of children's behaviour over recent years, with children resorting to tantrums and disruptive behaviour and being unable to express themselves adequately. It is unlikely that the limited early language skills of our youngest children as they enter school can be entirely blamed on technology. However all-day television, the demise of the family sit-down meal and maybe even forward-facing buggies could all be conspiring factors of the decline.

We exist in a society that values computer-screen navigation skills in our youngest children, if only so they are not disadvantaged when they come into contact with interactive whiteboards at most primary schools. This is an era where school children prefer ring-tone comparisons to playground sing-along games and one where university students can legally buy the successful academic work of others from the internet. Computer-generated games have replaced hand-drawn cartoons, the internet and online access have replaced books and libraries for many and we rely heavily on technology in every aspect of our lives. Many measure success technologically, by having the latest phone or gadget.

It must be remembered that technology is not technology to those who are born into an age defined by it. Nevertheless, a child's introduction to technology should be culturally and developmentally sensitive and begun only when a child's cognitive and conceptual autonomy has been established.

What does need to be avoided in education is the perpetuation of the expectation of always being provided with the answer, possibly fostering lethargy and a lack of effort in children. The best of all outcomes is when a child's innate intelligence is amplified by the use of technology rather than defined by it. When a child

Figure 9.1 *Their digital world*

enjoys empowerment from the competent engagement with their digital world they live in rather than mindless dependency on it and, more importantly, has developed their own intuitive feel for truth and concepts, they can then challenge technology when it fails them. '*At its core, education is a people process. Yes, youngsters need tools, but most of all they need people.*'[12]

Whilst we need to demonstrate confidence, curiosity and competence with technology, we need to remain attentive so as not to prevent children from developing the blocks of cognitive understanding. A simple example of this is when a child is taught to use the buttons of a calculator to provide the correct answer before they have grasped the cognitive concepts of simple mathematics. The disposition to want to learn is fundamental for their engagement with future learning and engagement with education, and calculating and understanding the answer for themselves is crucial. Technology cannot replace the accurate application of logical knowledge or wise judgement, nor ensure the development of the skills and dispositions for doing so.

Regardless of the interactive technological environment of the current era, there is no substitute for getting two minds in contact, as the abstract concepts that underpin much of what we know about the world are shared and reconciled as new concrete knowledge.

Challenges and dilemmas

Political priorities

In 2006, Ken Robinson offered a reminder that many of the policies made for families and their children are based on the perspectives of those in government and that politicians have '*designed the system (education) in their own image*'.[13] The current focus of government policy is one of dealing with the impacting consequences of necessary austerity measures: the last Labour government focused on perceived social adversity: poverty, neglect, dysfunction and abuse. Rather than address the social inequalities that perpetuate the 'otherness' that children grow up knowing, the political solutions to social inequality are based on an arrogance that 'they' are worse off and disadvantaged and need to be 'helped', whether it due to adversity or austerity.

The advent of Sure Start

The original and founding ideals of the Sure Start movement late in the last century and the subsequent children centres borne from it were clearly linked to providing high quality childcare services to the most disadvantaged families in our most challenging communities. The armies of professionals singularly tasked to improving the life chances of the young children of these families moved in to the sounds of trumpets and with controversial headlines. Less than ten years later, many are low-key networking satellite community centres for routine medical facilities. The fundamental service of providing nurseries and crèches within many of the centres are contracted out to local private provision as franchises, since there is not enough profit to be made to sustain the high quality childcare vision. The parochial business model approach did not capture the imagination of the local communities. So this became a very expensive exercise which demonstrated that nothing can replace human relationships for establishing the social behaviours that can nurture aspiration and life success for the next generation.

Providing a balance

Practitioners and the adults who inhabit the world around young children have a special role to facilitate a balanced representation of social status, class and social differences based on race, gender, culture and religion. Being aware and reflective of the impact their own values and beliefs can have on their perceptions of social roles and stereotypes is crucial. Practitioners have a duty to monitor their practice for influences that inhibit all children experiencing such a balance. Being effective in how to respectfully challenge another person's view can perpetuate habits of tolerance of others. It also models to children some of the essential communication skills that will help them develop an understanding of another person's perspective.

Epilogue

Above all, the early years should be enjoyable and be fun for all those taking part. The unique way young children see the world offers pleasure to them and to those around them. It is a time for freedom spent with those we love. A modern ideal, perhaps, that reflects a nostalgic time gone by, but many of the fundamental aspects of child development that transcend political frameworks and educational curricula are encapsulated in this sentiment.

The often unseen attributes of a well-rounded individual are usually the by-products of their experiences as children. To be kind to others, empathic of another's needs, be able to trust in others and in your own resilience are all things that cannot be directly taught by adults or school. The relationships that children experience during these formative years can define the templates and learned patterns for their social behaviour for life. Competent social interaction skills have their foundations rooted in the early bonds developed with others and the actions they make and the responses they receive. It is important to provide children with social freedom with adults, peers and with emerging language. Doing this encourages their developing autonomy and sense of self efficacy and self-worth as they experience the world responding to them. To gather experience of the impacts a child has on their world informs their later capacity for empathy, kindness and care for others.

We can only facilitate opportunities for children's social and moral development by offering respectful and reciprocal interactions with them in a timely way. The significance of language in how children communicate their ideas and feelings to those in the environment around them cannot be understated. The social and cultural context of children's early experiences and relationships determines many of the values and perspectives that inform their interactions for life. Again freedom, opportunity and space to practise these early patterns of social behaviour and language in safe, playful and responsive relationships with trusted adults and friends are crucial so that young children learn moderation and tolerance of themselves and others.

Every life experience is within a context: of the family we are born into and of the cultural influences and nuances that impact on our perceptions and under-standings of that context. Young children are social beings. Whether they become proficiently sociable is reliant on the relationships and language of which they have personal experience, often at the hands of the adults around them. Language has power over all of us, and we have a duty to employ it with care and purpose around young children. As do the social rules that they encounter, they need to make sense to young children and offer boundaries for communal behaviours that are beneficial for all. The rules of the wider world begin, for many children, at school.

Tolerance, kindness to others, empathy, an ability to make competent social judgements and build emotional resilience to life's inevitable knocks are all lessons we cannot teach. They are intangible, immeasurable and yet inherently desirable, for success as an adult social being. They are all by-products of a child's childhood experiences, of which we are an innate part.

We have a responsibility to the next generation to offer a wide variety of first-hand learning experiences to children, not only within the context of formal education, but also within the relationships and social interactions we are lucky enough to share with them. All these need to be with boundaries and social appropriateness applied, for our sake and theirs.

We have an educational culture that does not tolerate failure or vulnerabilities as well as it could. The system is target and outcome driven, with a social focus of bringing the ages, and not the stages, of children together. But we must not lose sight of the fact that failure and mistakes are at the core of all learning, and in particular, social learning. As humans hardwired to be social beings, being social is always hit and miss, since we can never really know the feelings or view of others. Mistakes of perception about another's perspective or values can cause intolerance, ignorance and indifference. All are at odds with the social traits that we may hope to encourage in our children. What we need to do is tolerate and allow the social mistakes that children make, past the culturally appropriate window for doing so.

Success in social relationships is centred on a willingness to have a go and being able to reconcile getting it wrong, and by being emotionally vulnerable to the responses of others. Children naturally do this. In a culture that stigmatises mistakes, developing genuine relationships that nurture a person's esteem and wellbeing means taking risks. Who is going to show our children how to do this?

This book hopefully continues to unravel some of the theoretical viewpoints that surround relationships and language in the early years and guides the reader through a practical, common-sense approach of how these can look in practice. It has endeavoured to provide and develop an awareness of the subtle, often unseen, influences on a child's social development. Any insights, knowledge and learning that heighten the awareness of the importance of children establishing healthy social relationships and the language to express their feelings and ideas effectively for their life-long wellbeing have to be a step in the right direction.

Notes

Introduction to the series

1 National Association for the Education of Young Children. Position statement, 2009.
2 DfES, *The Early Years Foundation Stage*. London: DfES, 2007.

Introduction to *The Social Child*

1 D. Whitebread, *Teaching and Learning in the Early Years*. London: David Fulton, 2003.

1 Setting the scene

1 J. S. Bruner, 'The Psychology of Pedagogy', in J. S. Bruner, *The Relevance of Education*. London: George Allen & Unwin, 1972.
2 *Nursery World*, May 2008.
3 *Fry's Planet Word*, Episode 1: 'Babel'. First shown 26 November 2011, BBC2.
4 M. Holmes, *What is Gender? Sociological Approaches*. London: SAGE Publications, 2007.
5 Bronfenbrenner's social model (1979) from P. Smith, H. Cowie and M. Blades, *Understanding Children's Development*. 4th edn. Oxford: Blackwell, 2005.
6 M. Holmes, *What is Gender? Sociological Approaches*. London: SAGE Publications, 2007.
7 B. Davies, *Life in the Classroom and the Playground*. London: Routledge & Kegan Paul, 1982.
8 H. R. Schaffer, *Introducing Child Psychology*. Oxford: Blackwell, 2004.
9 See K. Sylva and I. Lunt, *Child Development: A First Course*. Oxford: Blackwell, 1982.
10 S. Gerhardt, *Why Love Matters: How Affection Shapes a Baby's Brain*. London: Routledge, 2004.
11 Maria Robinson, 'Awareness', *Nursery World*, 22 May 2008.
12 L. Eliot, *Pink Brain, Blue Brain*. Oxford: Oneworld Publications, 2010.
13 Giordana Grossi (2010) in Eliot, *Pink Brain, Blue Brain*.
14 T. Bruce and C. Meggitt, *Child Care and Education*. London: Hodder & Stoughton Educational, 2002.
15 Mead (1962) in M. Holmes, *What is Gender? Sociological Approaches*. London: SAGE Publications, 2007.
16 R. Layard and J. Dunn, *A Good Childhood: Searching for Values in a Competitive Age*. London: The Children's Society, 2009.
17 B. Davies, *Life in the Classroom and Playground*. London: Routledge & Kegan Paul, 1982.
18 J. Newson and E. Newson, *Perspectives on School at Seven Years Old*. London: George Allen & Unwin, 1977.
19 BBC *Fry's Planet Word*, Episode 1 'Babel', screened 26 September 2011.
20 N. Postman, *The Disappearance of Childhood*. New York: Vintage Books, 1994.
21 J. Kenway and E. Bullen, *Consuming Children*. Berkshire: Open University Press, 2001.
22 D. Tapscott, *Growing up Digital*. New York: McGraw Hill, 1998.
23 P. Kirkham (ed.), *The Gendered Object*. Manchester: Manchester University Press, 1996.

24 T. Byron, 'Safer Children in a Digital World'. National Education Network Independent Review, 2008.

2 Play, imitation and exploration

1 J. Wood, *Gendered Lives: Communication, Gender, and Culture*. 5th edn. Belmont, CA: Thomson Wadsworth, 2003.
2 T. David, in K. Hirst and C. Nutbrown, *Perspectives on Early Childhood Education*. Stoke on Trent: Trentham Books, 2005.
3 D. Whitebread, *Teaching and Learning in the Early Years*. London: David Fulton, 2003.
4 S. Lester and W. Russell, *Play for a Change Review*. For Play England by National Children's Bureau, 2008.
5 C. Fine, *Delusions of Gender*. London: Icon Books, 2010.

3 Active learning; learning to be sociable

1 B. Davies, *Life in the Classroom and the Playground*. London: Routledge & Kegan Paul, 1982.
2 G. Claxton and M. Carr, 'A Framework for Teaching Learning: The Dynamics of Disposition', *Early Years* 24.1, March 2004.
3 V. Sherbourne, *Developmental Movement for Children*. London: Worth Publishing, 2001.
  D. Matsumoto, *People: Psychology from a Cultural Perspective*. California: Wadsworth, 1994.
4 D. Pennington, *Essential Personality*. London: Hodder, 2003.
5 I. Siraj-Blatchford and P. Clarke, *Supporting Identity, Diversity and Language*. Buckingham: Open University Press, 2000.
6 *Collins English Dictionary – Complete and Unabridged*. HarperCollins, 1991, 1994, 1998, 2000, 2003.
7 M. Foley, *The Age of Absurdity*. London: Simon & Schuster, 2011.
8 D. Elkind, *The Power of Play*. Cambridge, MA: Da Capo Press, 2007.
9 S. Gerhardt, *Why Love Matters: How Affection Shapes a Baby's Brain*. London: Routledge, 2004.
10 B. Rankin, 'The Importance of Intentional Socialization among Children in Small Groups: A Conversation with Loris Malaguzzi', *Early Childhood Education Journal* 32.2, October 2004.
11 Rankin, 'The Importance of Intentional Socialization among Children in Small Groups'.
12 http://www.baliadvertiser.biz/articles/teach_children/2007/loris.html. (Accessed November 2011)
13 R. Restak, *The New Brain*. London: Rodale Publishing, 2004.

4 Creating sociable language

1 B. Davies, *Life in the Classroom and the Playground*. London: Routledge & Kegan Paul, 1982.
2 H. R. Schaffer, *Introducing Child Psychology*. Oxford: Blackwell, 2004.
3 P. Connolly, *Boys and Schooling in the Early Years*. London: Routledge Falmer, 2004.
4 H. Bee and D. Boyd, *The Developing Child*. 10th edn. Harlow: Pearson, 2010.
5 From Bee and Boyd, *The Developing Child*.
6 From Bee and Boyd, *The Developing Child*.
7 From Bee and Boyd, *The Developing Child*.
8 S. Zeedyk and J. Robertson, 'The Connected Baby: A Film Conversation'. UK: The British Psychological Society, 2011.
9 K. Sylva, E. Melhuish, P. Sammons, I. Siraj-Blatchford and B. Taggart, *The Effective Provision of Pre-School Education*. DfES, 2003.
10 T. Bruce and C. Meggitt, *Child Care and Education*. London: Hodder & Stoughton Educational, 2002.
11 K. Sylva and I. Lunt, *Child Development: A First Course*. Oxford: Blackwell, 1982.
12 M. Quinn and T. Quinn, *From Pram to Primary*. Belfast: Co Down Universities Press, 1995.
13 Hugh Cunningham, *The Invention of Childhood*. London: BBC Books, 2006.

5 Seeing children talk

1 'Ken Robinson Says Schools Kill Creativity', TED Speech, 2006, held in Monterey California, at http://www.ted.com/talks/ken_robinson_says_schools_kill_creativity.html. (Accessed January 2012)
2 D. W. Winnicott, *Playing and Reality*. London: Tavistock, 1971, p. 51.

6 Engaging with families

1 J. Devereux and J. Miller, *Working with Children in the Early Years*. London: David Fulton Publishers, 2003.
2 I. Siraj-Blatchford, 'Educational Disadvantage in the Early Year: How do we Overcome it? Some Lessons from Research', *European Early Childhood Education Research Journal* 12.2 (2004), p. 5.
3 *The Early Years Foundation Stage*, London: DfE, 2012.
4 DfES and Department of Health, *Every Child Matters: Change for Children*. Surestart Children's Centres Practice Guidance. Dept of Education and Schools, 2007.
5 P. Hughes and G. MacNaughton, 'Consensus, Dissensus or Community: The Politics of Parent Involvement in Early Childhood Education', *Contemporary Issues in Early Childhood* 1.3 (2000), p. 241.
6 Hughes and MacNaughton, 'Consensus, Dissensus or Community', p. 241.
7 B. Lipton, *The Biology of Belief*. London: Hay House UK, 2005.
8 Cited in Lipton, *The Biology of Belief*.
9 DofE, *Statutory Framework for the Early Years Foundation Stage – Setting the Standards for Learning, Development and Care from Birth to Five*. London: Dept of Education, 2012.

7 Embracing differences

1 L. Eliot, *Pink Brain, Blue Brain*. Oxford: Oneworld Publications, 2010.
2 M. Holmes, *What is Gender? Sociological Approaches*. London: SAGE Publications, 2007.
3 J. Wood, *Gendered Lives: Communication, Gender, and Culture*. 5th edn. Belmont, CA: Thomson Wadsworth, 2003.
4 Wood, *Gendered Lives*.
5 H. R. Schaffer, *Introducing Child Psychology*. Oxford: Blackwell, 2004.
6 Eliot, *Pink Brain, Blue Brain*.
7 P. Hammond, 'I Want Everything Now!' *Eye* 9.2, June 2007.
8 Wood, *Gendered Lives*.
9 Julia Donaldson, *The Gruffalo*. London: Macmillan, 2011.

8 The links of language

1 N. Stadlen, *What Mothers Do*. London: Piaktus Books, 2004. S. Gerhardt, *Why Love Matters*. East Sussex: Routledge, 2004.
2 M. Whitehead, *The Development of Language and Literacy*. London: Hodder & Stoughton Educational, 1996.
3 J. Blanden, 'Bucking the Trend: What Enables those who are Disadvantaged in Childhood to Succeed Later in Life?' Working Paper No 31, Dept of Work and Pensions: Crown Copyright, 2006.
4 M. Whitehead, *Supporting Language and Literacy Development in the Early Years*. Buckingham: Open University Press, 1999.

9 Ready for school, prepared for life?

1 'Ken Robinson Says Schools Kill Creativity', TED Speech, 2006, held in Monterey California, at http://www.ted.com/talks/ken_robinson_says_schools_kill_creativity.html. (Accessed January 2012)
2 Department for Education and Employment, *Schools: Building on Success*. London: The Stationery Office, 2001.

3 Department for Education and Skills, *Schools: Achieving Success*. London: The Stationery Office, 2001.

4 J. Russell, 'Let's Put Character Above Exam Results', *The Sunday Times*, 5 June 2011.

5 C. G. Mooney, *Theories of Childhood: An Introduction to Dewey, Montessori, Erikson, Piaget and Vygotsky*. USA: Redleaf Press, 2000.

6 Hartshorne and May, from L. Nucci, 'Moral Development and Character Formation', in H. J. Walberg and G. D. Haertel, *Psychology and Educational Practice*. Berkeley: MacCarchan, 1997, pp. 127–57.

7 Nucci, 'Moral Development and Character Formation', pp. 127–57.

8 Cited in I. Siraj-Blatchford and P. Clarke, *Supporting Identity, Diversity and Language in the Early Years*. Buckingham: Open University Press, 2000.

9 DofE Research Brief RB134, p. 25.

10 Education for All Global Monitoring Report, at http://www.unesco.org/education/GMR/2007/chapter2.pdf. (Accessed July 2012)

11 R. Layard and J. Dunn, *A Good Childhood: Searching for Values in a Competitive Age*. London: Penguin Group, 2009.

12 T. Oppenheimer, *The Flickering Mind*. New York: Random House, 2003.

13 'Ken Robinson Says Schools Kill Creativity', TED Speech, 2006, held in Monterey California, at http://www.ted.com/talks/ken_robinson_says_schools_kill_creativity.html. (Accessed January 2012)

Author index

Subject index